UNCHAIN YOUR BUSINESS

How to let go and grow

Nick Bettes

CONTENTS

"Paying attention to simple little things that most men neglect makes a few men rich." – Henry Ford

PROLOGUE: WHY BUSINESSES GET STUCK

If you are reading this then you are probably responsible for leading a Small or Medium Enterprise (SME), either as an owner, partner or director. Running your own business can be exciting, challenging, rewarding and lucrative.

However, it isn't always like that. Many SMEs fail (Hart & Anyadike-Danes, 2014). Few achieve their full potential (Anyadike-Danes, 2010). Most grow for a while and then reach some plateau where, despite the best efforts of the business owner, they continue to bump along year after year.

Why is this?

It is tempting to blame external factors. The market turned down. The economy got worse. I can't get the staff. This rather comforting viewpoint might be undermined by looking around you; well-run businesses thrive whatever the external environment is.

Usually the problem with your business is straightforward. It's in the mirror. The limiting factor for most businesses is the time, attention and knowledge of the person or group of people running it. By working hard, for long hours, the owners grow the business – perhaps for many years. But there comes a point where every new thing they must do means that something they used to do doesn't get done. Even though the business might employ more staff, overall productivity seems to have gone down.

Managing a business and leading people is a difficult thing to do well. Large successful companies spend huge amounts of time and money training people to do this. Yet somehow the leaders of SMEs are expected to develop the skills of a chief executive on their own by trial and error.

Would you fly on a plane where the pilot was learning by trial and error? Or go under a self-taught surgeon's knife? Of course not. And whilst business is not usually a matter of life or death, your business is probably a really big part of your life and core to your economic wellbeing. Nevertheless, the vast majority of SME managers expect to "pick it up as they go along" – and equally a significant number of businesses struggle and then get trapped. This is not coincidence – these facts are related.

This book describes how you can run your business differently and break out of this trap by making it scalable and less reliant on you. The first chapter explores why businesses stall in this way using a cautionary parable, Smiths Widgets. Subsequent chapters describe how these problems can be overcome by applying a process called systemisation. At the end we return to Smiths Widgets to see whether they find a way out of the trap.

Note: You don't have to take my word for it. At the start of each chapter are a few words from business owners who have already changed their business and the way they run it using the systemisation techniques described in this book.

So...the hero of our tale is having a torrid time and is running a stalled business. He doesn't know this yet – he thinks he can work his way out of it – but he can't because he is trapped. He's an amalgam of many business owners I have worked with and he and his partner have their fair share of problems...

CHAPTER ONE: SMITHS WIDGETS, FOR EXAMPLE

Systemisation in practice: RH, owner of an audio-visual reseller, says: "[systemisation]...has been extremely productive [...] and has resulted in significant improvements in the way my business operates, directly affecting retained bottom line profit. [...] concept of the process driven business with clearly defined systems and processes is a breath of fresh air."

When John Smith launched the business, it was mainly because he didn't think much of the way his previous employer went about things. He didn't enjoy working for someone else and felt frustrated because it often seemed he wasn't given enough time to do the job as well as he wanted to. John was sure that there was space for a business that produced better widgets than anyone else. He also thought he could see an opening for a brand new kind of widget. He felt he was the best widget maker around - and nothing has happened since to change that point of view.

He's managed to hire half a dozen other widget makers in the six years he's been running the business. They are all pretty good at it in their own way – but John is proud that he is still the best at it. He still has to get involved whenever there is a tricky job – the company can't afford any mistakes.

The staff he has hired are a good bunch on the whole, and the business would certainly not have grown to where it is without them. The additional administration is a real pain though. John knows that his job is to make and sell widgets but the more staff he gets the more time he has to waste on explaining things and on controlling everything they do. Fortunately, he's managed to resist setting up the monthly management reviews that his accountant suggested by asking her to email through the monthly accounts. He started his business to make great widgets, not to waste time in meetings. He knows that managing a business is just something you can pick up along the way – it's not as if it's a real skill like making widgets.

John started out without too much in the way of a clear purpose and strategy for the business but then, so did most business owners he knows. Since then, the business has evolved pretty well. Work comes in and invoices are sent out and people get hired. John spends his time on the important things; selling, delivering and getting paid - although he's noticed increasing amounts of his effort going on dealing with staff. Occasionally he reads about the need for a strategy and feels slightly uneasy, particularly since taking on Andrew Brown as a partner a couple of years ago. The one time he and Andrew did try to discuss the long-term plan it was a bit dispiriting – embarrassing even. They weren't really sure how to go about it and it almost seemed as if the two of them had different pictures of the future. Luckily both John and Andrew are happier getting stuck in than sitting back thinking about the future. As long as they keep reacting quickly to opportunities and the work keeps coming in, they reason, who needs a strategy? Obviously, everyone involved knows what the business is about anyway.

Smiths Widgets must be doing something right – the company is getting chances to pitch for new and bigger clients – even if they haven't won any yet. It's turning out to be tough to explain to these new prospects why they should take Smiths' products. It would be great if the company could just stick with the couple of clients they've had since the start - they just get it, it doesn't take loads of meetings to make a sale. John sometimes thinks about just focusing on these clients but can see that they just won't deliver the growth the company needs – that's why the sales figures have flattened out over the last couple of years. So they keep on trying different ways of marketing – networking, website, leaflets, radio ads, a different special offer every month. They figure that some of it will stick, more prospects will get to hear about the amazing features of the new Widge-o-matic and orders will follow.

When John started the business, he had to do everything himself. A couple of the people he has picked up since then are real assets who know the way their bit of the business works inside-out. That really helps when something goes wrong and they have to pull out all the stops to get the right result.

As Andrew has said, the great thing is with this team is that you don't need to write things down in procedures, or measure how well things are going. No-one has time to do that, anyway – always too busy getting orders out of the door, or launching the next marketing campaign, or putting the latest fire out. Curiously, even though they've recruited quite a few people over the years, it now seems to be getting more difficult to find good staff. They've tried hiring a few new people recently, but they were pretty unproductive – none of them seemed able to pick up the way things work around here, or figure out what they needed to do. Most of them didn't stay long so now John and Andrew just plan to cope with the people they have, at least in the short term.

One thing that was supposed to help them do this was putting in the new order management system. This was John's baby. He had hoped it would improve efficiency and increase capacity but so far no-one really understands how to use it – or wants to use it - and neither John nor Andrew have had time to figure out what the reports mean anyway. Until they find time to start using the system properly, they have resigned themselves to working even longer hours. They are pretty sure that they can get a bit more out of the staff as well, although they are going through a bit of a sticky patch with them at the moment. One of the longest-serving employees left last month and another one has had quite a bit of sick time recently. Last time he was off no-one else knew how to pick up the project that he had been dealing with and that caused a few problems.

John sometimes wishes it was just him and his original couple of staff again. In those days, everyone could do everything, and everyone mucked in without complaining. They were more like friends than employees. They all went for a drink sometimes after work and he felt that they shared his ambition for the business. Now he's got employees that he feels he doesn't know very well. He likes all of them, but they don't seem to care as much about the business – it's really just a pay packet to them. He seems to spend more time listening to them complain about things and telling him their problems than he does getting them to do useful stuff. To be fair, all the staff are willing enough workers once they are given a task – but John finds himself spending more and more time on detailed instructions and more and more time checking up on how they are doing it in order to avoid mistakes.

It would help if some of the staff were willing to take the initiative on tasks, but this seldom happens, despite the fact that John has allowed plenty of room for innovation by not tying them down with job descriptions, clear objectives or reporting lines. John and Andrew hope that their own innovative mindset will rub off on the staff in time; they are both constantly coming up with new ideas, each more critical than the critical task given to an employee a few days ago.

Sometimes if he is really pushed for time, John will try delegating tasks by handing a problem over to someone and telling them to do what they think best. Usually, however, he tries to avoid this as it always ends up badly and he ends up doing it himself anyway!

Last year, John and Andrew tried to improve morale by holding a couple of team meetings and even had a go at appraisals but both initiatives took a lot of time that they felt could have been spent on doing something more useful. For his part, John felt a bit of an idiot standing up in front of all the employees or asking someone how they enjoyed their job. The whole thing was rather a negative experience so neither of them is sorry that they have been too busy to repeat the process since.

CHAPTER TWO: SYSTEMISED BUSINESSES ARE DIFFERENT

Systemisation in practice: SH, owner of an electrical contractor, says: "We have seen a quantifiable increase in sales, our systems and processes are more efficient, and we now have higher trained, more motivated staff. [...] comprehensive analysis of all areas of our business has enabled us to restructure the way we work, enabling a focus on our business goals."

Even though the story of Smiths Widgets is something of a caricature, it is based on real experiences with real clients and it illustrates the four things that are always completely or partially missing from businesses that stall. These are:

1)   The Correct Mindset
2)   A Shared Purpose
3)   Repeatable Processes
4)   Accountable Employees.

Systemising your business is a way of building these four things into your business. They are interdependent and reinforcing so all four changes must be made.

Businesses that achieve this are not only bigger and more scalable – they are fundamentally different.

THE CORRECT MINDSET

The first step to systemising your business is to recognise the limiting beliefs that are holding you back and replace them with enabling beliefs:

> *"No-one else can do this as well as I can"*

If this is true, you don't have a business. What you have is a job with a supporting cast whose role is to make you look good. You need to replace this limiting belief with an enabling belief that it is your role to develop people to be better at what you do than you are.

> *"The most valuable thing I do is make widgets (or build houses, or websites, or write contracts, or mow*

> *lawns, or develop software) – time spent doing other things, especially learning how to manage, is time wasted"*

If this is your belief, you will never progress much beyond being self-employed. You need to replace this limiting belief with an enabling belief that your job is to build a business, acquiring and mastering all the skills necessary to achieve this. You employ other people to do the doing.

> *"Employees should do what they are told"*

They might do, for a while. They will probably comply. Successful businesses, however, are built by employees who are engaged, who share a vision of something that is worth doing and that is bigger than them. You need to replace this limiting belief with an enabling belief that your job is to build a compelling vision that engages all your employees.

> *"I must control everything. I can rely only upon myself, not on my employees"*

If this is the way you want to behave then either your business will forever be limited to those few people and things that you can handle at once, or you will make yourself ill trying to control more than is physically possible, or both. You need to replace this limiting belief with an enabling belief that your role is to delegate everything and delegate well. Your role is to enable your staff to succeed. Your role is to build trust and capability in your staff to do the right things and make the right decisions.

> *"People only work for money"*

If you think your staff only come to work to get paid – they *will* only come to work to get paid. If you believe that they are mercenary and short-sighted – they *will* be mercenary and short-sighted. You need to replace this limiting belief with an enabling belief that you must pay people enough – but challenge, achievement, self-reliance and purpose drive real motivation and productivity.

> *"My aspirations must be realistic"*

If you have a meagre vision or are prepared to accept the status quo then you can be sure that your achievements will not exceed this – and that your staff will not be inspired to excel. If you have a bold vision that you truly believe in then you may not achieve it – but your staff will be motivated by the vision and your belief in it...and who knows? You need to replace this limiting belief with an enabling belief that your business can be a world-beater and you know that your staff believe in you and in the vision.

A SHARED PURPOSE

Without a clear purpose you, your business and your staff are drifting on an ocean buffeted by waves of random events. Without a clear purpose you have no chart, sail or compass – and nowhere to set course for even if you had.

Purpose is multi-faceted. It includes a destination – a compelling vision of what things will be like. It includes a vehicle – a description of the way that you intend to travel, what you believe in, what you value, what you do - that resonates with employees and customers. It includes a map – the strategy that explains what is different about your offering, how it is a better proposition for your chosen market.

It includes your Core Engine of Growth - an explicit description of how you take a pound or dollar of profit and put it back into the business to generate two more pounds or dollars of profit.

It includes milestones: Strategic objectives that focus your efforts, keep you on course and tell you what progress you are making.

Having a purpose means that your business is more likely to survive and thrive. You have made explicit a strategy that makes the most of your strengths, the market opportunities and your opponents' weaknesses.

Having a purpose means that your customers are more likely to buy. You have identified your market niche and focused your marketing on it. You have refined your proposition so that it uniquely addresses their exact needs.

Having a purpose means that your employees are engaged. They understand what you are trying to achieve and are drawn to the things your business stands for. They feel themselves part of something bigger than themselves. They are proud to be part of it.

Having a purpose makes your life simpler. It guides your decision-making, telling you which course to take and which to avoid. It provides a focus that draws you on.

REPEATABLE PROCESSES

Processes make your business efficient, repeatable, resilient, reliable and scalable.

They capture and document the things that your business does to turn one pound into two, or one dollar into five. They identify how the performance of your business is measured using Key Performance Indicators (KPIs). They set targets for these to match your strategic objectives (your purpose). Individual roles are captured in job descriptions that match processes, or tasks within processes.

Establishing processes identifies and eliminates bottlenecks, delays and inefficiencies. It gives your employees the tools and resources they need to excel. It may implement new computer systems, or it may simply show you how to make the best use of your existing ones. It uses your systems to provide the measurements you need to delegate, develop staff, drive sales, understand marketing, improve cash flow - in short, to manage your business.

It removes as far as possible the reliance on any one person, including you, the owner. It de-mystifies what individuals do and the resulting transparency makes teamwork possible. Having cover, or being able to cover roles quickly, makes the business more resilient and flexible. It allows you to hire staff with a high level of confidence that they will be able to perform their duties well and get up to speed quickly because, in a systemised business, employees have manuals, useful and relevant computer systems, job descriptions, measurement and feedback, development plans and a supporting routine.

Establishing processes lets you make comparisons and so initiate improvements. You can compare across time periods, across people, across products, across teams and across customers.

In a systemised business you can get things done through others. You can describe what they need to achieve, measure their progress and provide guidance – without having to micro-manage or intervene at every step. Your time is released to drive business development.

In a systemised business you can measure and improve. You can drive business performance because you understand the machine. It is no longer a collection of disconnected people and events. You can see the dials and pull the levers.

Established processes produce a better, more reliable experience for customers. You can produce the same result for them every time.

ACCOUNTABLE EMPLOYEES

People are much easier to manage when they are committed to the cause. They are also much more productive. Instead of just turning up to work and complying with instructions they give discretionary effort. They go the extra mile.

An engaged workforce is aligned with the organisation's purpose. They feel pride in being part of a winning team and teamwork comes naturally to them as a result.

Engaged employees take responsibility. They are accountable for their own actions. They take ownership of problems and are empowered to come up with solutions.

Developing an engaged, accountable workforce requires action on two levels. The first level, the platform for engagement, is comparatively mechanical and controllable. It is formed by implementing things such as clear reporting lines, relevant job descriptions, individual objectives, strong management routines, appraisal systems and staff development plans. Job descriptions are based on unambiguous accountability for measurable outputs. People are made responsible for achieving appropriate targets and given adequate tools and resources to achieve these. Performance is managed through robust management routines and regular appraisals.

The second stage, to build engagement on top of this platform, requires consistent, fair, predictable leadership, a compelling and well-communicated vision, appropriate employee autonomy, and continuous staff development.

You and your managers must walk the talk, demonstrating under all circumstances the values and behaviours you want your staff to adopt. The vision is developed as part of the purpose of the organisation and this, with values, forms the backbone of an internal communication process. Increasing autonomy for your staff is prepared for by appraisals and personal development plans (to develop the necessary skills) and achieved through delegation (to give them the opportunity to practice and learn).

CHAPTER THREE: CREATING A SYSTEMISED BUSINESS

Systemisation in practice: JB, owner of a financial services business, says: "[systemisation]...helps me to find what is important for our business and what is not[...]We now have proper systems in place, reliable data that all our team can use and most importantly a clear vision of where we are going[...]It is no coincidence that we are closing our best business month ever."

WHERE DO I START?

I suggested in the previous chapter that the four components are interdependent:

- Your management mindset that expects people to be accountable, connected to a purpose that incorporates a clear and compelling vision, and to efficient, well-organised processes, encourages staff accountability to flourish;
- Productive, self-motivated accountable staff, connected to processes with reliable performance measurement, and to clear purposeful objectives, means that staff take on ownership of tasks and allows you the owner the time, confidence and support to further develop your business growth mindset;
- A well-defined, purposeful market definition and proposition allows you to implement solid repeatable delivery processes and set relevant, engaging goals for staff...and so on

Conversely, if your mindset is that of a self-employed worker rather than that of a business owner then you will struggle to define a true purpose for others. If you have no clear purpose, then how will you systemise your processes to deliver it? If you have frustrating, inconsistent processes and no clear purpose then you cannot expect employees to start taking responsibility.

So successful systemisation is powered by you developing a systemisation mindset. It all starts with you changing what you believe, say and do. You might consider this a big ask; reinvent my management self, based purely on faith? Change the habits and beliefs of a lifetime in business based purely on a few words in a book?

Fair enough. I need to demonstrate some benefits. I'll help you make a couple of changes as proof. The Baselining section in the next chapter walks you through choosing what these first changes should be. However, getting started does require a commitment from you to change the way your business works. You need to set and achieve some objectives that you believe will produce material improvements in your business. Your systemisation mindset will develop as you see the benefits of systemisation on the ground, in your business.

WHERE DO I END UP? WHAT DOES A SYSTEMISED BUSINESS LOOK LIKE?

A systemised business produces consistently good quality results regardless of the people involved on any given day or how busy you are. Results for customers, such as lead time or errors, are measured. The processes that produce the results for customers are documented and repeatable. Someone in the business owns these things and is measured against them.

A systemised business runs on management routines. Plans and performance are reviewed at weekly operational meetings, monthly management meetings and quarterly strategy meetings. These meeting are efficient because they make use of the correct management information. These meetings take place regardless of what else is happening in the business.

A systemised business produces boring cash flow, not exciting surprises. Surprises in business are bad. Uncertainty undermines action. The systemised business is controlled using a live business plan. This means fewer unforeseen problems, and hardly any self-inflicted ones.

The leader of a systemised business spends their time creating and developing a vision and selecting, coaching and empowering staff to achieve it. The leader strives not to do anything. They have a delegation plan, which sets out who is going to be doing those few things that the leader still does. There is an effective framework for delegation in place which includes an organisation chart, job descriptions, key performance indicators and objectives.

Employees in a systemised business are accountable for business results. Every employee has at least one number (KPI) for which they are responsible. These numbers are documented and agreed in the employee's annual objectives. Performance at the top level is reviewed every month in the management review meeting, and annually with individual employees in an appraisal.

Systemised businesses have documented processes and make effective use of information systems. The business has an Operating Manual that sets out how things are done. Information systems are used to reduce cost, speed processes up and differentiate the product or service.

Systemised businesses have a clear vision and strategy which is understood by all employees. The business has a One-Page Strategy that has been created with the input of all employees. The key elements of that strategy are discussed during recruitment, performance reviews, team meetings, appraisals and every time success or failure is encountered.

Systemised businesses are managed using numbers. The business uses a dashboard (also called a KPI Sheet or Live Plan), to run the monthly management review. Every KPI belongs to someone at the meeting.

BUT WHAT DO I ACTUALLY DO TO SYSTEMISE MY BUSINESS?

Every business is different, of course, but during my work with dozens and dozens of systemisation clients I have identified fourteen business changes that systemising businesses typically need to make. These changes are set out in The Systemisation Roadmap (Figure 1). The Systemisation Roadmap is used to assess your start point (what do you have or are you doing well already; what is missing or a problem) and priorities (what is the most critical thing to achieve).

The Systemisation Roadmap then helps you identify the changes you need to make and the ideal sequence you need to make them in. It is also used to keep track of progress.

The essence of systemisation is getting things done through others (your employees) so that the business can move beyond the things that you can directly do or control yourself. The key to this is developing a shared understanding amongst all employees of the following four things:

1)   What (are we trying to achieve)?
2)   Who (does what)?
3)   When (do things need to be done)?
4)   How (do we do things)?

The following section gives a brief description of each of these fourteen changes that together allow you to get things done through other people. In subsequent chapters I describe in detail how to go about making these changes.

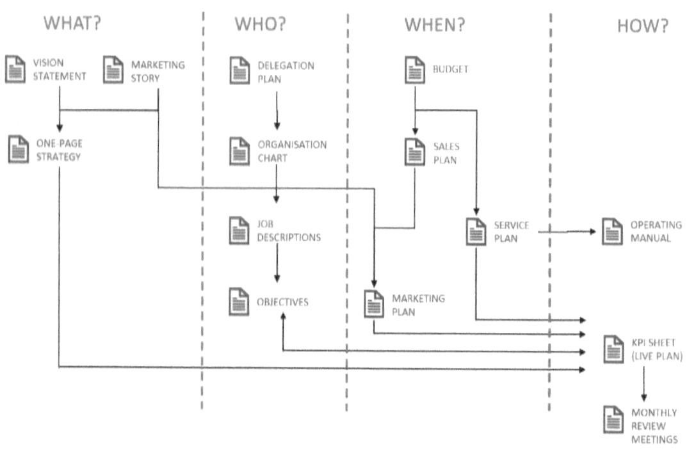

Figure 1 - The Systemisation Roadmap

THE FOURTEEN CHANGES

Your Vision Statement

Creating your Vision Statement forces you to examine and clarify what you want to achieve through owning your business.

Involving your employees in creating this provides them with a clear and motivating sense of purpose

Your Marketing Story

For marketing to work you must be crystal clear about:

1)   Your niche
2)   Their pain, need or want

3) Your solution, and why it is better than anyone else's

Your Marketing Story captures this and is used as the basis for all your marketing, digital and real-world, as well as key parts of your sales process.

Your One-Page Strategy

The purpose of creating a strategy is to communicate purpose and direction to investors and employees and to keep this purpose and direction clear before you.

Effective communication needs to be simple and concise. The One-Page Strategy forces you to distill your complex view of the business into this simple and concise message.

Your Delegation Plan

Delegation is an essential technique for successfully distributing the tasks that you perform currently to the employee who should be doing them. This is a key step in making your business scalable.

Your objective should be to delegate everything you do. Your delegation plan sets out how and when this is going to happen.

Your Organisation Chart

The process of formalising an appropriate structure will force you to address inconsistencies, gaps and duplications – and to consider how effective your people and processes really are.

Defining structure leads naturally to defining outputs and so helps accountability.

Growing and changing the business requires clear reporting lines and responsibilities.

Your Employee Job Descriptions

Job descriptions are an essential part of making employees accountable for results.

Without a job description an employee does not have a clear understanding of what they are supposed to achieve and how their performance is measured – and you have no way to hold them accountable.

The process of creating and reviewing job descriptions is an opportunity to discuss and clarify the role – to reinforce two-way communication.

Your Employee Objectives

Strategic objectives and KPI targets are delivered by people having individual accountability for them.

They allow you to communicate what is required of an employee and measure whether it has been achieved. They usually form part of a performance management system, being set and reviewed annually.

They provide purpose, context and a sense of achievement for the employee.

Your Budget

Delegation, accountability and performance requires a plan. Business planning starts with numbers - your Budget.

Building a simple financial forecast covering three years and matching your vision or strategic goals allows you to get the business planning process started. The numbers provide a spine for the plan and drive marketing, sales and production figures and KPIs.

The summary numbers from your Budget go on to your KPI Sheet.

Your Sales Plan

The Sales Plan turns the revenue line of your Budget into required sales activities and outcomes.

It defines your sales process from enquiry to sale together with the ratios and lead-times across each stage. It also sets out how you manage existing accounts to maximise revenue from them.

In this way it defines your sales KPIs such as average order value and sales pipeline value.

Your Marketing Plan

Your Marketing Plan connects your new sales and account development targets to marketing activities.

You use it to set out the forms of marketing you are going to employ, the money and time you are going to invest in each and the return (number of enquires) you expect.

It defines your marketing KPIs, such as average cost per lead.

Your Service Plan

Your Service Plan explains what resources are required to deliver the planned revenue. This could include, for instance, call-centre agents, field service engineers, workstations, lathes, vans – anything that forms a significant part of your cost and whose numbers can if necessary be adjusted over the life of your plan.

Setting productivity and utilisation targets or norms helps you understand how many resources you need and how they need to be managed to maximise long-term profitability.

Your Service Plan also includes customer-facing KPIs, such as delivery time and error rates.

Your Operating Manual

Delegation, efficient operations, great customer service and profitable growth require a consistent and proven process which delivers the same result with the same quality time after time. This must be maintained no matter how busy you are and no matter how fast the company grows.

You cannot rely solely upon individual knowledge and motivation to achieve this. People get sick or leave. Steps are skipped or forgotten during busy periods. Word-of-mouth or on-the-job training for new staff is an ineffective means of transmitting crucial knowledge about how the required results are achieved.

For all these reasons it is essential that all the key processes in the business are documented, publicised and accessible.

Your KPI Sheet

Key performance indicators (KPIs) are the few (six to eight) vital measurements that tell you whether your business is going in the right direction or not. Typically, these will include financial, marketing, sales and service numbers.

They form a dashboard for your business.

Your KPI sheet shows the targets for the next 12 months and the actuals for the last 12 months.

Your Monthly Management Review

The Monthly Management Review brings your management team together to review performance and agree actions.

It is based on the KPI Sheet.

It is the forum to develop the people who will run the different parts of your business into a high-performing team.

CHAPTER FOUR: GETTING STARTED - BASELINING

Systemisation in practice: RA, owner of a PR company, says: "[systemisation]...has provided the perspective that we need to make better and more objective decisions about operation and growth. I would recommend [...] to anyone trying to get the most out of their business."

In the following chapters we will work through the detail of how you make these fourteen changes to your business.

Books are linear, so I have had to choose a logical sequence in which to present these changes. You will see I have chosen to start with vision, which is the place many of my clients start. Of course, businesses are not linear, or even very logical. They are unique, multi-dimensional and work only if the awkward carbon-based lifeforms that populate them choose to make them work.

In practice, systemisation may start in several places at once. Some elements may already be in place, some elements may be revisited several times during the process and some may just not get done. Most changes have a bearing on other changes – the work done in implementing job descriptions may lead you to revisit your Budget, for instance, or your delegation plan. You may decide to start where you believe you have an able manager who is in tune with what you are trying to do - just to get some traction.

Leadership is about communication. Only through effective communication will you get your people to march in step with you. Effective communication is two-way; you must be interested in what others have to say. Every change presented in the following fourteen chapters is an opportunity to communicate with your employees. If you take nothing else from this book, remember the most powerful four words in management: "What do *you* think?".

In order to promote this communication, each chapter is presented as exercises designed to be run with your key employees. To maximise interaction and involvement each exercise is designed to be done by a small group of attendees and then presented to the rest of the room in a show-and-tell session. However, I recommend that, to start with, you simply read the book, working through the material in splendid isolation, before starting work for real with your employees.

When you are ready to involve them, you can download predefined templates for each exercise from the resource website given at the end of the book.

While you run each exercise, your aim is to understand and incorporate the opinions of your employees, but it is your business and you need to find a way to include your own thinking in the results. You can either join in and do each exercise yourself or you can use the show-and-tell discussion at the end of each exercise to feed your own ideas into the process. You should consider whether an external facilitator would make the process more effective - business owners have a tendency to dominate and their employees have usually been trained to believe the boss is always right.

Note: There is an implicit trade-off throughout this systemisation process. If you want your staff to be more engaged, share your sense of purpose and take responsibility for results then you must face up to ceding some control. By this I mean that you must be willing to give up your untrammeled power to make unilateral decisions about your business, and instead become more consultative, more prepared to listen to employees and let them take bigger decisions.

Please don't try to systemise your business by starting with the first section (Your Vision Statement) and working your way all the way through to the last section (Monthly Management Review), applying to your business every tool, template and guide as you go. I don't want to be responsible for the medical, recruitment and divorce bills you will incur as a result. Instead, use the Baselining section that follows to decide where you are going to begin and the first few changes you are going to make.

Finally, even though this book presents systemisation as a series of steps it is essential to think of systemisation as a continuous, iterative approach; a new way of running your business, not as a one-off project.

BASELINING

Baselining is where you set your systemisation goals and priorities and develop your initial action plan.

Current Situation

If you have got this far in the book, I imagine that you are being motivated by some frustration about the way your business is running. It will help to plan your systemisation efforts if you take the time to clarify this frustration. Here are some real situation statements from some of my clients:

> *"I am working too many hours"*
>
> *"My staff are not very productive"*
>
> *"I have never been able to grow the business past x employees or y revenue"*
>
> *"We are not very good at adding new customers"*
>
> *"We are delivering late more frequently and with more defects"*

You can use the Systemisation Roadmap to look for changes that might have a bearing on these statements (and your own situation statement) and so suggest a start point that might help. For the above this might be:

> *"I am working too many hours <u>because</u> I am unable to delegate things" (Delegation Planner)*
>
> *"My staff are not very productive <u>because</u> I have no way to manage their performance" (Organisation Chart, Job Descriptions or Employee Objectives)*
>
> *"I have never been able to grow the business past x employees or y revenue <u>because</u> I always run out of time to do everything that needs doing as we get bigger" (Delegation Planner)*
>
> *"We are not very good at adding new customers <u>because</u> we don't really do marketing or sales very well" (Marketing Story)*
>
> *"We are delivering late more frequently and with more defects <u>because</u> we have grown and our processes are no longer fit for purpose" (Operating Manual)*

Note: In these examples, arriving at these situation statements and possible start points for these clients required some listening and questioning by the consultant (me) – see the chapter "Successful Systemisation".

Creating your own situation statement will help you articulate your desired state.

Desired State

Successful change needs a clear vision of the world after the change – your desired state.

To give up smoking a smoker must have a compelling vision of herself and her new life as a non-smoker.

To win an Olympic medal the athlete must have a vision of themselves on the podium that is compelling enough to get them out of bed at 4am for training every day of the week.

You should have no more than three goals and they should be simply stated:

> *"I want to be spending only two days a week in the business in two years' time"*
>
> *"I want to double revenue by date x"*
>
> *"I want a functioning management team in place by date y"*
>
> *"We want all our key processes to be documented and their performance being measured by the end of the year"*

The acid test is that you should have a timescale for each goal and its achievement should be unambiguous. In the examples above the phrases "functioning management team" and "key processes" need a little more precision.

Defining your own systemisation goals will help you decide your priorities for change.

PRIORITISING

Your situation statement and systemisation goals should indicate your own start point on the Systemisation Roadmap.

You can see that the roadmap shows some dependencies; it would be difficult to complete your One-Page Strategy without having a clear Marketing Story, for instance. However, these dependencies are not cast in stone and the whole process is iterative. If you needed to, it would be perfectly possible to start by creating someone's job description without having an Organisation Chart for example. However, you do need to give some consideration to sequence. If your goal is to build a great marketing and sales operation but you are currently working sixty hours a week controlling production, you might need to fix delegation first just in order to free up your time to fix sales.

If you are stuck, you might want to consider the following broad approach based on the default start points implied by the diagram:

- If you feel that there is no common purpose or direction amongst employees and that this lack of context will make it difficult to engage staff in your systemisation initiative, then start with your Vision Statement;
- If you feel that you are the bottleneck in most things and that your own time is so taken up by doing things within the business that it will leave you no time to progress with systemisation, start with your Delegation Planner;
- If you feel that weaknesses in your marketing and sales efforts will mean that revenue and cash concerns will distract you from systemising your business, then start with your Marketing Story;

- If you feel that your business has no plan or budget and that this will make it difficult to control and plan any changes then start with your Budget.

Once you have identified the first few changes you want to make, use the relevant following chapters to guide you through making these changes.

CHAPTER FIVE:
YOUR VISION
STATEMENT

OVERVIEW

In this section you will develop your Vision Statement.

This will provide you and your employees with a clear and simple purpose for the organisation. Involving your employees in defining this purpose means that they will feel a sense of ownership and engagement in what you are trying to achieve.

I recommend that you create your Vision Statement in a workshop with your key staff using the Vision Workshop Agenda below. The exercises will help you and your staff challenge current assumptions, generate alternative views of the future, reach consensus around the most desirable of these and identify what needs to change to make it happen.

Allow three hours for the workshop. Here is a suggested agenda (each exercise is described in the following pages):

Vision Workshop Agenda

1) Introductions (if necessary)
2) Objective (To develop a shared vision for the business as a basis for strategy and internal communication)
3) Exercise – Scenarios
4) Exercise – Visioning Tool
5) Exercise – Shared Vision
6) Exercise – Tailwinds and Headwinds
7) Summary and close – next steps (discuss vision with employees and run a marketing workshop)

SCENARIOS

The Scenarios Exercise in Figure 2 is used to generate alternative possibilities and to avoid making assumptions or sticking to historical perspectives on your business. As with all such brainstorming approaches, avoid being critical or analytical at this stage and let the ideas flow.

Depending on the knowledge of attendees you can now either work through the "Current" column with them as a group (using a flip-chart or white-board) or simply ask them to complete this column themselves. The completed column should give a snapshot of your business today. Typically, you will have turnover and net margin in the finance row; a list of your main product lines in the next row (perhaps with some indication of relative importance); a list of the main customer types in the next row and so on.

Now ask attendees to come up with three different scenarios or future pictures of the business. Give them a timescale (three or five years are often chosen). You will probably need to prompt them by suggesting, for example, "What if we had more branches?", "What if we were providing a much better service to customers?" or "What if we were selling something different?". Encourage them to be as off-the-wall as possible. Attendees should describe three scenarios, one in each column, using the dimension given in the left-hand column.

Finally, ask each attendee in turn to describe one of their scenarios to the group. Go around the group until you have captured the key points from all scenarios on a flipchart, endeavoring to identify common themes and significant differences.

Dimension:	Current	In 3 years		
		Scenario 1	Scenario 2	Scenario 3
Financial				
Products and services				
Market sectors, typical customers				
Other (people, geography, systems, structure...)				

Figure 2 – Scenarios Exercise

After the exercise make sure you retain the summary flipcharts from the show-and-tell session for use when completing your Vision Statement.

VISIONS

Now ask each participant to use the ideas generated by the scenario exercise to start generating their vision. This forces them to select what they think will be the "best" scenario (usually some combination of plausibility and benefit) and start thinking about details and timelines.

Give each participant an exercise sheet (see Figure 3) and ask them to complete it. Start with the 3-years column. Make sure you use numbers wherever possible to avoid woolliness – "Our business will be bigger" is not a very useful vision. If necessary, change the timescale at the top. You can also complete the first column (how things are now). Completing the 12-month column is then just a matter of interpolating between your current and desired state. This should start to bring home the things that you need to get started on quite quickly.

Dimension:	Current	In 12 months	In 3 years
Financial			
Products and services			
Market sectors and customers			
Reputation or brand			
Marketing activities and capability			
Sales process and capability			
People and organisation			
Systems and procedures			
Management and leadership			

Figure 3 - Vision Exercise

A SHARED VISION

Ask each participant in turn to talk through one row of their Vision Exercise results. On a flipchart capture the key points and then move on to the next person. Use a separate flipchart for each dimension (Products and services, Marketing capabilities and so on) but try to get everyone's thoughts on that topic on the one sheet. Highlight themes and differences as you go.

You are trying to draw out a vision that aligns with your thoughts but captures the insights of the workshop and the thoughts of the attendees.

When all dimensions and attendees have been covered try to summarise in a few sentences the shared vision that is emerging. Highlight the key elements on each chart and get someone to capture these on a separate flipchart or blank Vision Exercise template. After the exercise make sure you retain these summary flipcharts or completed template for use when completing your Vision Statement

HEADWINDS AND TAILWINDS

Now you can start to think about the changes or actions necessary to achieve your Vision. The Headwinds and Tailwinds exercise is useful for this.

Give each participant a blank exercise sheet (Figure 4) and ask them to complete it.

Ask them to briefly summarise the main points from the Vision Exercise in the first box - give it a name if it helps capture the essence of your vision.

Ask them to list, in the tailwinds column, the factors (internal or external) that will help you achieve the vision - for example, strong market growth or a new product. In the headwinds column list the factors that will hinder its achievement, for instance difficulty in recruiting staff or obsolete technology. Ask them to identify the initiatives or changes you will need to make to take advantage of the former and ameliorate the latter.

In the show-and-tell session capture the positive and negative factors and required actions identified by each person on flipcharts. Retain these for completing your Vision Statement.

<table>
<tr><td colspan="2">Vision:</td></tr>
<tr><td>Tailwinds ===>>></td><td><<<=== Headwinds</td></tr>
<tr><td></td><td></td></tr>
</table>

Figure 4 - Headwinds and Tailwinds Exercise

COMPLETING YOUR VISION STATEMENT

To complete this stage, you need to turn the results into a proper Vision Statement. Look at the example in Figure 5. Often the most difficult but most critical part of this whole exercise is turning something rather fragmented and detailed into a simple, compelling purpose for your staff. In many ways the essence of the leadership role is to communicate simple, compelling visions of the future to employees, so this is a great opportunity to practice this.

You will need to refer back to the summary flipcharts from the workshop to complete this.

In three years' time Acme Trading will have revenues of £5,500,000. We will have maintained gross profit margins at today's level but improved net margin to 18%.

We will be employing 60 staff and have a dedicated business development function which will include a channel partner network. The business will be run by a management team; each manager will be responsible for achieving agreed business targets.

We will have launched a subscription version of our product and this will account for 40% of revenue. This will allow us to extend our sales geographically and enhance our reputation for providing the most cost-effective solutions in our marketplace.

Improved employment and management practices will have resulted in an employee satisfaction rating that increases year on year over this period.

Figure 5 – Example Vision Statement

Once you are happy with your Vision Statement make sure you discuss it with all your employees. No matter how proud of it you are, don't present it to them as a polished, finished item. Instead make sure it looks like a work in progress and *ask them what they think*. Then make your final adjustments.

The result should be, as the story goes, something that you can communicate to someone in a lift journey between floors which is so compelling that they want to invest in your business – whether that is their money or their career.

Email everyone a copy of the final thing. From now on you should refer to the Vision whenever possible – when hiring, praising, celebrating success, raking through the ashes of something that went wrong, reviewing performance, doing appraisals and so on – in order to bring it to life. Only repeated story-telling and examples over years will start to make your Vision your employees' vision as well.

> ### *I've Done the Vision*
>
> *Early in my work with the Managing Director of a field service firm I suggested that developing a shared vision might help his staff understand what he was trying to achieve and perhaps make them feel more a part of that journey.*
>
> *When I returned a month later, he announced "I've done the vision". Sure enough, there were copies of a vision document placed on every desk and pinned to noticeboards. I asked how he had engaged his staff in discussing and shaping his vision and he looked surprised. "I haven't got time to do that – nor have they. I just wrote it myself." he replied.*

> *Deep breath. Accept that my communication must have been pretty poor in the previous session. Repeat the session but from a different perspective and with new stories.*

CHAPTER SIX: YOUR MARKETING STORY

OVERVIEW

In this section you will develop your Marketing Story.

For marketing to work, everyone in the business must understand the sector or niche you serve, what problem or need your product solves and how it is better than the competition's.

Developing your Marketing Story achieves this. The result is used as the basis for all your marketing and sales.

I recommend that you start to develop your Marketing Story by running a workshop with your key staff using the Marketing Story Workshop Agenda shown here.

Marketing Story Workshop Agenda

1) Introductions (if necessary)
2) Objective (To draft the Marketing Story for the business as a basis for strategy and business development)
3) Exercise - My Market Niche
4) Exercise - My Customers' Pain
5) Exercise - My Proposition
6) Summary and close - next steps (Complete Marketing Story, discuss with employees and run a strategy workshop).

NICHE

Start with the Marketing Niche Exercise in Figure 6. The point of this is to get beyond superficial classifications and build a more detailed picture of your ideal client.

Before you do this exercise, a word on customer categories:

Customer Categories

What are customer categories?

- Too many companies define their target market too broadly – "consumers" is a common description, as is "SMEs" or even (slightly better) "the construction industry"
- You need to divide that market down further into more narrowly-defined types of customer, for example:
  - o "Owner-managed businesses in the RG postcode with between 5 and 50 employees" or
  - o "Builders on the local council suppliers list who do not have an internal H&S manager" or

- o "Women between 25 and 35 who are fashion-conscious but on a budget."
- It helps to give them a name – for instance a supermarket chain might categorise some of its customers as "Brand Loyalists" and others as "Pie-and-Mashers". These are sometimes called "customer archetypes"
- A customer category is another way of describing a market niche

Why have customer categories?

- It will help you make decisions about which customers you want – and which you don't want.
- Which customers are more profitable – and which are a nightmare to deal with?
- It will help you understand why those customers choose your product or service – or that of your competitors:
  - o Which benefits are more important to them – and which less?
  - o How well do you match those desires – and how do you compare with the competition?
- It will help you develop propositions which are tuned to the customers' requirements – even if the base product or service is the same.
- It will help you quickly and easily communicate the type of customer you are looking for.
- You should strive to be number 1 or 2 in your market. If you are not big enough to achieve this in the whole market you can focus on a niche (a customer category) where you can be number 1 or 2 and so dominate.

How do you identify customer categories?

- Think through the benefits that your customers are seeking – what is important to them and how does it differ for different customers?

- Think about the different ways they buy – where, when, how often?
- Think about different attributes – age, sex, where they live
- Think about the different things your product or service does for different customers:
  - What need does it fulfil?
  - What does it allow them to deliver to their customers?
  - What barriers does it remove?
  - How many different uses is it put to?
  - Ask them!
- Take the differences that you find most useful and group them into customer categories.

Now run the exercise. Follow this with a show-and-tell, capturing the results on flipcharts. Don't forget to retain these for use in creating your Marketing Story.

Your market niche is the market sector, or the kind of customer, you focus on.

Individually, use post-it notes to list down as many attributes of your best or ideal customers as you can (one attribute to each post-it). Think about geographic factors (where they are), demographic factors (how old, what sex (if you sell to consumers) or how many employees (if you sell to other businesses)) and psychographic factors (what do they like or avoid?). Even if you sell to other organisations don't forget it is still people who buy from you. What is their title? What kind of people with this title are your ideal customers?

Don't edit your thoughts at this stage; put every attribute down. When everyone has run out of ideas take it in turns to read out your notes then start to group them into common factors. From this try as a group to come up with a few sentences that captures these factors as a description of your ideal customer.

Write this description on a flipchart and be prepared to explain it to the facilitator or the other groups.

Figure 6 – Marketing Niche Exercise

CUSTOMER PAIN

Using the niche you identified in the previous section, ask attendees to work through the My Customers' Pain Exercise given in Figure 7. This exercise again forces you to think more deeply about the underlying logical and emotional reasons for your niche needing your product. You should find that understanding and defining the pain gives you new insight into your niche.

Now run the exercise. Follow this with a show-and-tell, capturing the results on flipcharts. Don't forget to retain these for use in creating your Marketing Story.

> Your customers' pain (or desire) is the problem that your product or service addresses.
>
> Individually, use post-it notes to write down all the pains and desires that your customers think your product or service addresses. Note that you need to think beyond the core product. For instance, if you sell printers then your customers pain is not "I want to print things" but perhaps "I am spending too much on printing and they are always breaking down".
>
> Don't edit your thoughts at this stage; put every attribute down. When everyone has run out of ideas take it in turns to read out your notes then start to group them into common factors. From this try as a group to come up with a few sentences that captures these factors as a description of your customers' pain or desire.
>
> Write this description on a flipchart and be prepared to explain it to the facilitator or other groups.

Figure 7 - My Customers' Pain Exercise

PROPOSITION

Now you can start to think about how your product or service is uniquely designed to be the best fit for this pain by working through the Your Proposition Exercise in Figure 8. As with the previous exercises, thinking deeply about this will repay you with a better and more useful outcome.

Before you do this exercise, here is a word or two on the thorny issue of Unique Selling Propositions (USPs).

Your Unique Selling Proposition

What is a USP?

- Your USP is the collection of attributes that makes your offering stand out in the market.
- It must be:
  o A tangible difference
  o Relevant (the attribute must matter to the customer)
  o A better fit to the pain your customer is feeling
  o Simple and easily communicated
  o Hard to copy
  o Provable
  o Based on something that you do differently – your unique process or secret formula.
- It is NOT EVER just "service" or any other platitude.
- It can be price – if your processes deliver a sustainable cost advantage.

Why have a USP?

- It will help you arouse interest in your offering.
- It will help you build barriers between your customers and your competitors.
- It will help you charge more and avoid competing on price:
  o If you are just a me-too company, what else can you compete on except price?
  o If you have something different that people want, then they have to come to you.
- It makes you more memorable.
- It will help you quickly and easily communicate the essence of what you do.

How do you develop your USP?

- Think about why your customers buy from you instead of someone else.

- Ask them!
- Understand the benefits they receive (not the features you offer).
- Find out which benefits are critical to the purchase decision.
- Think about the things you do differently from the competition – these may or may not matter to the customer, but they are worth investigating.
- Think about the things that you do that you would not want to outsource or sub-contract. How does doing this thing add value from the customer perspective? For instance, manufacturing in house might allow faster delivery.
- Think about the things that you own or use to deliver the service that others would find difficult to acquire (including knowledge, location or venue). How does owning these things translate into value from the customer perspective?
- Make sure you think about the process (the customer experience) and not just the result (the service or product).
- Verne Harnish in his book "Scaling Up" (Harnish, 2014) talks about "Words you own". Thinking about the words that you absolutely must dominate on Google might help you understand your USP.

Some Generic USPs to Get You Started

Price

- This can be low price if you have a unique process or advantage that will always keep your costs below that of the competition. If not, then competing solely on price is suicide.
- This could be high price if you have a luxury product which is in demand by people who want to be seen as able to afford exclusivity.

Speed

- This can be fast (for example food or deliveries) as long as you have a process which always delivers faster than anyone else.
- This could be slow (for example fine dining or whisky) as long as the wait is seen as part of the pay-off for the buyer.

Newness

- In the technology or gadget market some people buy things simply because they are new. Some businesses compete on performance (for example computers or phones) so they need innovation from their suppliers.
- Oldness can also be a selling point – think antiques, or retro, or reliability.

Convenience

- Petrol stations can charge more for essential items than supermarkets because they are next to the road and have parking. Convenience could also mean opening hours or home delivery or anything else that makes it easier for the customer.
- Being a one-stop shop.

Range

- Both breadth of range and numbers stocked can be a powerful USP. If a customer is pushed for time or in a fix they look for the place that always has what they need on the shelf.

Expertise or specialism

- The ultimate is to be seen as a specialist in a field of one. This is really what defining a niche is about; making yourself a specialist.

Quality and Service

- This is never just the word "quality" or "service", but a deep understanding of what attributes represent quality and service in your market and a proposition which not only delivers on these attributes but uses descriptions of them to resonate with the customer.

Reliability

- This is about understanding your prospects' deepest fears about your product and addressing them through a unique guarantee, your longevity or testimonials.

Now hand out the exercise sheet below. Ask attendees individually to complete the following table noting if and how the factors contribute to your USP. When everyone has finished conduct a show-and-tell session. Identify common factors and on a flipchart produce a few sentences that describe your USP.

Don't forget to retain this for use in creating your Marketing Story.

Price (high or low)	
Speed (fast or slow)	
Newness (or oldness)	
Convenience (or inconvenience)	
Range	
Expertise or specialism	
Quality or service (but NOT those words)	
Reliability	
Other	
Other	
Other	

Figure 8 – Your Proposition Exercise

COMPLETING YOUR MARKETING STORY

Finally, you need to turn the results of these three exercises into your Marketing Story using the Your Marketing Story Exercise (see Figure 9). The example in light type in the exercise is concise; you will probably have a lot more words (and a lot more flipcharts) than this at this point. Once again, the most difficult but most critical part of this whole exercise can be turning something rather fragmented and detailed into a simple, compelling story for your staff and customers. I hope that you are beginning to understand that the essence of the leadership role is to communicate simple, compelling visions of the future to employees, so this is another opportunity to practice this.

You should use all the flipcharts you have retained from the workshop sessions to complete this sheet. Don't try to cram everything in - focus on the core elements.

Your strapline – what you do	*Example: "We insure things that are difficult to insure."*
Your niche – who your customers are	*Example: "Our customers are householders in areas prone to flooding or other catastrophe."*
Their problem – what they need	*Example: "They find it impossible to get adequate insurance at a reasonable price."*
Your solution – how you help and why it is different and better	*Example: "Our unique database and brokerage network means that we can insure the most difficult properties quickly and cheaply."*
The result – after buying your product or service how is their life better?	*Example: "As a result our clients are able to sleep soundly in their beds and get on with their lives knowing that they are secure should the worst happen."*

Figure 9 - Your Marketing Story Exercise

The answers should flow together to make a story.

All successful businesses have a differentiated proposition – but this USP only makes sense in the context of a well-defined niche and a particular set of circumstances (the problem, need or want).

Your business may have several different niches and propositions – each one requires its own Marketing Story.

This Marketing Story can be used to develop everything from your elevator pitch to your website; it should underpin every element of your marketing.

Once you are happy with your Marketing Story find a way to discuss it with all your employees. Remember, don't present it to them as a finished item because they will not feel able to engage with or challenge what you are saying. Present it as a work in progress and *ask them what they think*. Afterwards make your final adjustments.

The result should be a sound basis for action. Review (or have someone else review) all your marketing materials (digital and physical) in the light of this new story. Revise things as necessary, not forgetting that you are looking for a simple compelling message whether that is a leaflet, a website, a sales script or a social media campaign. Avoid the temptation to throw the kitchen sink at these things – in marketing, less is more, so strip things back to your Marketing Story.

Email everyone a copy of the final thing. From now on you should refer to the Marketing Story whenever possible in order to bring it to life. Only repeated story-telling and examples over years will start to embed your Marketing Story in the minds of your people.

> *"When I hear the word 'culture', that's when I reach for my revolver".*

> *Like Goering, I am suspicious of some words. Whenever a client tells me that they compete on "customer service" or "quality" I know that they don't really know what they are competing on.*
>
> *If they tell me that they win business based on "their relationship" it is worse – not only do they not know what they are competing on but what they have is completely non-scalable without cloning since it relies on their unique and magnetic personality.*
>
> *Platitudes are no substitute for doing some difficult, rigorous thinking. The idea is not just to tick the box marked "USP" but to identify a meaningful, defendable difference and then use it to beat the opposition to a pulp.*

CHAPTER SEVEN: YOUR ONE-PAGE STRATEGY

OVERVIEW

In this section you will create your One-Page Strategy.

Your strategy sets out how you are going to compete in the marketplace in order to deliver the vision. It is created to communicate this to employees, shareholders and customers; keeping it to a single page forces you to simplify and focus on the essence of this communication

Involving your staff in creating the strategy means a) they are more likely to understand and believe in it and b) you will get a better strategy.

I recommend that you start this with a workshop with your key staff using the Strategy Workshop Agenda shown below.

The agenda suggests some exercises using standard strategic tools; it is not necessary to use all of them (indeed, you could replace them with other tools). None of the models are correct or real – you can think of them as "tools for thought". The idea is to use these firstly to generate different perspectives on your business and how to achieve your business aims and secondly to promote discussion and debate in order to engage your staff in the process and the result.

You will almost certainly run out of time - a good sign as it means you have achieved engagement and discussion. It does not matter if the last exercise is skipped.

One-Page Strategy Workshop Agenda

1) Introductions (if necessary)
2) Objective (To stimulate the thinking and provide a sound basis to develop a One-Page Strategy for the business as a basis for business planning and internal communication)
3) Recap on the Vision Statement and Marketing Story
4) Exercise - SWOT and PEST
5) Exercise - The Competitive Landscape
6) Exercise – Competitive Factors
7) Exercise - Values Audit
8) Summary and close - next steps (document the workshop key points using the One-Page Strategy template as a guide then discuss with all employees)

REVIEW VISION STATEMENT AND MARKETING STORY

Start by reminding people what your Vision Statement and Marketing Story say. Don't open these things up for discussion again but people who weren't at the previous workshops need to understand the foundation of your strategy (and it is just conceivable that people who *were* there may be a little hazy about details).

The key points to get over are where the business is going and what customers it is going to serve to get there.

SWOT AND PEST

The SWOT and PEST Exercise (Figure 10) is designed to help you assess how well your business is set up to achieve your vision. What capabilities provide the secret formula that underpins your proposition? Which things are you less good at and will this undermine your chances of success? What impact, either positive or negative, will the choppy seas around you have on achieving your vision?

Ask attendees to complete the table below. Explain that the point of this exercise is to take action to address the insights generated. How can you mitigate the negatives and take advantage of the positives? What vital few actions do you need to take? Make sure those parts of the form are completed.

		Strengths		Weaknesses	
INTERNAL		*Actions*		*Actions*	
		Opportunities	Threats	*Actions*	
EXTERNAL	Political/ Legal				
	Economic/ Environmental				
	Social				
	Technological				

Figure 10 – SWOT and PEST Exercise

In the show-and-tell session that follows, encourage people to challenge any assumptions. For instance, "a strong brand" is often trotted out as a strength. Who says so? Compared with which competitors? Define "strong". Similarly, something along the lines of "Our great employees" is often dropped into the mix. This needs to be approached with a little more circumspection but again, says who? How do we know? How is this measured? In what way does this allow us to beat the competition? SWOT and PEST analysis has developed a bit of a poor reputation in recent years; this is not the fault of the tool but of rigour-free and superficial usage.

During this session collate people's ideas onto a flipchart for each area (one for "Strengths", one for "Weaknesses" and so forth). Identify common themes and make sure you capture the actions that mitigate weaknesses or threats or build on opportunities or strengths. Failure to do anything about the issues thrown up by the analysis other than stick them in a strategy document has contributed to the tool's decline.

Retain these summary sheets - you will need them to complete your One-Page Strategy.

COMPETITIVE LANDSCAPE

The Competitive Landscape diagram and Exercise given in Figures 11 and 12 is designed to give you an alternative perspective on your business environment. Part of developing a strategy is to examine the competitive landscape and think about how it might evolve over the life of your strategy and how you might influence this or take advantage of it.

The landscape includes your partners and suppliers and the people who specify or integrate your product or service as well as your customers.

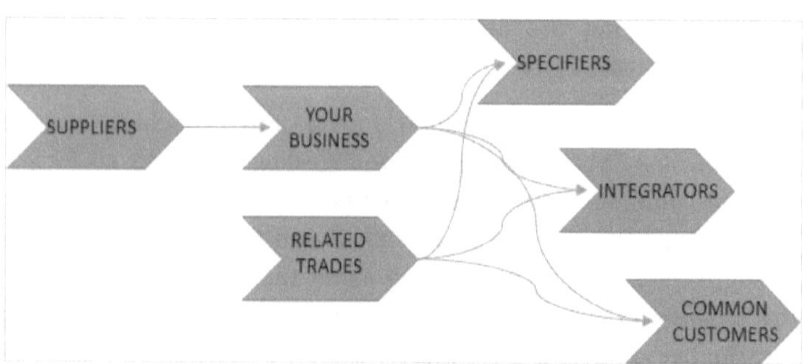

Figure 11 - Competitive Landscape

This landscape is not fixed. Value moves as markets, needs and technologies evolve. Organisations acquire new or dispose of existing capabilities. Links between stages are bypassed as different delivery systems evolve.

As with any tool like this we need to simplify things. If you provide multiple product types to multiple sectors it will be easier if you limit this exercise to one or a subset of these.

Ask attendees to complete the table given in Figure 12 and then present their insights and conclusions about how this landscape is likely to change and how you should respond. Use flipcharts to capture key insights and actions and retain these - you will need them to complete your One-Page Strategy.

Which companies provide products or services that my customer needs to get benefit from my product or service?	
Which of these companies would the customer find it most difficult to change as a supplier? How is this going to change over the life of our strategy?	
How much overlap is there between our capabilities and those of these related companies? Could we do what they do or they do what we do?	
Who are our main suppliers?	
Do our suppliers have a choice of customers like us? Do we have a choice of suppliers like them?	
How difficult would it be for our suppliers to bypass us and serve our customers direct? How is this going to change over the life of our strategy?	
Do our customers rely on specifiers? If so	
How do we increase our power over specifiers? How is transparency affecting this?	
Is the power of specifiers likely to change over the life of our strategy?	
Do we sell to or via integrators? If so	
How do we limit the power and margin of integrators?	
How difficult would it be for us to become an integrator? Would this increase or decrease margins?	

Figure 12 – Competitive Landscape Exercise

COMPETITIVE FACTORS

This exercise asks you to use the tool shown in Figure 13 to look at your competitors and your comparative strengths and weaknesses. How does your proposition and secret formula fit into this? Is it positioning you in new ground with a distinctly different offering?

To use the tool, list the factors on which competition takes place in your market in the first column - for instance "Price" or "Availability" or "New functionality". Indicate in the boxes where your main competitors focus their proposition - for example if Competitor A focuses on low price then put an "A" in the "5" column for the Price factor. If Competitor A is less focused on new functionality then put an A in the "2" column, say, for this factor. Once you have plotted Competitor A across all factors then do the same for all your main competitors or competitor types and then plot your own positioning. How does this help you think through your own (different) proposition? Where are you competing differently from everyone else? Where are the gaps in the market that you could move into?

For the show-and-tell prepare two or three flipcharts with the layout in Figure 13. Ask people to explain what they had as competitive factors and try to come up with a consolidated list. Then ask each person to add your company's profile to the flipchart. Finally ask everyone in turn to plot a competitor or competitor type on the chart as well (you can see why you might need two or three sheets for this!)

Retain these summary sheets - you will need them to complete your One-Page Strategy.

COMPETITIVE FACTORS	← LOW	IMPORTANCE TO THE PROPOSITION			HIGH →
	1	2	3	4	5
(EG PRICE)					
(EG SPEED)					
(EG RANGE)					

Figure 13 – Competitive Factors Exercise

VALUES AUDIT

The Values Audit Exercise (see Figure 14) asks you to decide whether your values and beliefs as a company will support your strategy. For instance, if you have processes and rewards focused on profit and your new strategy is focused on customer service then you are going to struggle to execute, not only because the mechanisms are wrong but also because few of your existing staff will have been hired for their customer service excellence. Before you look at the exercise here is a brief note on the importance of strong values and beliefs within an organisation:

Values and Beliefs

Values and beliefs are core to what motivates people. They are deeply held and don't change significantly over time. Given the chance, people will spend their time on activities that match and reinforce these values. If what they spend their time doing is incongruent with these beliefs then they will experience dissatisfaction and stress and will try to change their environment, withdraw or go somewhere else.

For an organisation the implications are significant:

- Articulating and living up to a strong set of values and beliefs is a powerful way to engage with employees who also subscribe to those beliefs.
- If employees do not share the organisational values and beliefs, then they will not commit to the purpose of the organisation and performance will never achieve its potential.
- If employees' values and beliefs conflict with those demonstrated by the organisation then job satisfaction and performance will be low while staff attrition will be high.
- If an organisation's espoused values and beliefs are not matched by the actual behaviours, rewards, sanctions and controls in practice then employees will become confused, cynical and disloyal.
- Staff attitude and beliefs about the organisation, good and bad, will quickly be transmitted to customers and prospects and from there to financial performance.
- Organisations will over time attract employees who match their actual practised values and repel those who do not – regardless of what the organisation's espoused values are.
- Similarly, organisations will over time attract customers who match their actual practised values and repel those who do not – regardless of what the organisation's espoused values are
- A business strategy or initiative which does not match the real values and beliefs of the organisation is probably doomed to failure – but one that does match them will have the support and understanding of the employees.

What do you do about this?

- Firstly, understand your own values and beliefs. What is important to you? Wealth? Technical excellence? Creativity? Integrity? Helping others? Trusting others? Make sure your business vision, your strategy, what you produce and how you go about it matches these.
- Next, understand the value sets of your senior team. If they are materially different from your own does this strengthen or weaken your top team? Create a teambuilding process that means you all share the same objectives for the business and believe in the strategy.
- Where are your values and beliefs made concrete for your employees and customers? Review your processes, reward systems, marketing messages and actions to ensure that they reinforce the values and beliefs that you want for your company.

Now give all attendees a copy of the Values Audit Exercise. Ask them as individuals to identify their core values and beliefs in the first column, numbering the most important "1", the next most important "2" and so on up to 5. This tells you the things that matter to your current employees. Next, take a similar approach to the second column, asking them to identify the five things that they feel will be critical to successfully following your strategy. Some of these things will have been identified in previous exercises. Finally, complete the third column. This lists the implicit values currently demonstrated by the organisation. These can be derived from the key performance indicators, the behaviours that are rewarded and discouraged, the things that you the owner focus on (and ignore), and the actual experience of customers and employees.

Note: The show-and-tell for this can be sensitive and you need to consider whether an independent facilitator should run the exercise – and whether you should be present. You might get a more useful result if you are not.

For the purpose of your strategy you are interested in the answers to two questions:

1) Is there a gap between the answers in the first and second column? Are the things valued by your employees congruent with the things you all need to believe in to succeed with your strategy? If not, what needs to change and how?
2) Is there a gap between the second and third columns? Are the things that the organisation actually believes and values congruent with what is required to execute your strategy and achieve the vision? If not, which needs to change, and how?

Capture the key points of the discussion on a flipchart and retain this to complete your One-Page Strategy.

	The things that you value most are:	The things that the strategy implies the organisation values most are:	The things that the organisation demonstrates it values most are:
Achievement & reputation			
Career & personal development			
Change & adventure			
Community & belonging			
Competence & quality			
Controls, procedures & standards			
Creativity & innovation			
Customer service			
Having fun			
Helping others			
Income & wealth			
Independence & empowerment			
Integrity & honesty			
Knowledge & expertise			
Loyalty			
Organisation & structure			
Personal health			
Power & prestige			
Profit			
Recognition			
Self-motivation & drive			
Stability & security			
Teamwork			
Technical excellence			
Work/life balance			

Figure 14 – Values Audit Exercise

COMPLETING YOUR ONE-PAGE STRATEGY

Having run the workshop and gathered the results, capture and summarise these using the One-Page Strategy guidelines in Figure 15.

<table>
<tr><td rowspan="2">Summary of Vision Statement</td><td rowspan="2" colspan="2">In three years Acme Insurance will have revenues of £5,500,000 and net margin of 18%. Growth will come from focusing on the high flood-risk sector. We will be employing 60 staff and have a channel partner network delivering 40% of revenue. A further 40% of revenue will come from online sales.</td><td colspan="4">Headline figures</td></tr>
<tr><td></td><td>Year 1</td><td>Year 2</td><td>Year 3</td></tr>
<tr><td></td><td></td><td>t/o</td><td>4.5m</td><td>4.9m</td><td>5.5m</td></tr>
<tr><td></td><td></td><td>Net margin</td><td>15%</td><td>17%</td><td>18%</td></tr>
<tr><td></td><td></td><td>Employees</td><td>48</td><td>55</td><td>60</td></tr>
<tr><td rowspan="4">Our Marketing Story</td><td>Niche</td><td colspan="5">Our target customers are householders in council tax bands C to E who live in flood-prone areas</td></tr>
<tr><td>Pain</td><td colspan="5">They have difficulty getting insurance</td></tr>
<tr><td>Proposition</td><td colspan="5">We will be able to offer them cover using our unique flood-mapping software and services from our flood-proofing partners</td></tr>
<tr><td>Our secret formula</td><td colspan="5">Flood prediction & impact software system. Risk-reduction using flood-proofing measures.</td></tr>
<tr><td rowspan="3">Market</td><td>Size</td><td>250,000 houses</td><td>Growth</td><td>20%</td><td>Our % share</td><td>12%</td></tr>
<tr><td>Main competitors</td><td colspan="5">Large insurers</td></tr>
<tr><td>Key drivers and changes</td><td colspan="5">Increasingly extreme weather, withdrawal for key players from market</td></tr>
<tr><td rowspan="3">Our values and beliefs</td><td colspan="2">The kind of people we are</td><td colspan="3">Accountable, supportive, ambitious</td></tr>
<tr><td colspan="2">Things that are important to us</td><td colspan="3">Happy employees, satisfied customers, growth, profit</td></tr>
<tr><td colspan="2">How we behave</td><td colspan="3">Love customers, respect each other, hit targets, keep promises</td></tr>
<tr><td rowspan="3">The vital few changes we are going to make</td><td colspan="5">1. Release 2 of the main system live</td></tr>
<tr><td colspan="5">2. Implement online sales</td></tr>
<tr><td colspan="5">3. Recruit channel sales team and set up partner network</td></tr>
</table>

Figure 15 – Example One Page Strategy

I have included example text as this is a crucial stage and a difficult one. I hope you have retained all the results from the workshop exercises to be distilled into this document. Once you are happy with it then, once again, make sure you discuss it with all your employees. Even if you think it is perfect, don't present it to them as the polished, finished item. Instead make sure it looks like something they can still change and *ask them what they think.* Afterwards, make your final adjustments.

> ### *Lions Don't Wear Suits*
>
> *I attended a corporate management conference once where the Marketing Director had, at some expense, produced small folding guides to our strategy. These were glossy, double-sided, close-printed affairs that set out in some detail the way that the organisation was going to survive and thrive. They were designed to fit into the breast pocket of a suit or a pocket in a handbag. Clearly the expectation was that we would take them out and refresh our memory when things were quiet, or perhaps produce them with a flourish when cornered by baffled employees or doubting prospects.*
>
> *We had a guest speaker at the event who was a South African former big game hunter who now lectured on strategy, taking as his theme the successful strategies of the kinds of animal he had, in his previous existence, shot at.*
>
> *By accident or design he made the point that members of a pride of lions do not have or need "...a card with their strategy written down.". This comment has always stuck in my mind, and not only because of the picture of the Marketing Director looking crestfallen in the front row amidst general tittering around the auditorium.*

> *Strategy is above all about communication. There is no point having a brilliant strategy if the troops cannot understand or remember it.*
>
> *Keep it simple.*

CHAPTER EIGHT: YOUR DELEGATION PLAN

OVERVIEW

In this section you will create your Delegation Plan.

Mastering delegation is a critical step to systemising your business. Your business cannot grow while you personally are essential for carrying out any tasks, making any non-strategic decisions or controlling the work of others.

Your objective is to delegate everything so that you can spend your time on developing the business. Once accountability and tasks have been delegated properly once then they can be delegated again – so your business suddenly becomes scalable.

This won't happen overnight and might take several years but it is more likely to happen if you follow a plan.

> *NOTE: I suggest you review the section "Plan the Change" in the "Successful Systemisation" chapter before embarking on any of the changes in the next four chapters. These are going to affect your staff and most of them won't like it. Before you change anything, I suggest you consult with your HR advisors to ensure you make these changes in accordance with the law in your country.*

THE DELEGATION PLANNER

We are going to use the Delegation Planner (Figure 16) for this project. Use it to list out all the things you spend your time doing. You may need more than one sheet! Don't edit your thoughts at this stage – you can always redo a tidy version of the plan later.

Activity	Time consumed	Criticality and difficulty[1]	Person who should be doing this[2]	Is this person ready, willing and able to take this on?	Is the process docu-mented?[3]	Does the process have defined measurable outcomes?[4]	Target dele-gation date	Actions required

Notes:
1. Be honest about this – invoicing might be critical, but it is not difficult, for instance
2. Use the organisation chart, accountability list and job descriptions to decide this
3. This might include checklists, quality criteria, decision-making rules, flow-charts and so on
4. You must be able to define success. This measurement might be a KPI for your business already

Figure 16 – Delegation Planner

PRIORITISING THINGS TO DELEGATE

Once you have your list start to prioritise the tasks, starting with the things that consume most of your time but that are neither critical nor difficult. Figure 17 provides a way of thinking about this.

Figure 17 - Prioritising What to Delegate

Estimate how much of your time each item takes, either in one go or in many smaller episodes. Then decide how critical and difficult each task is. Invoicing, for instance, is critical but it is not difficult and could be taught. Defining strategy however is both critical and difficult to teach and so it is probably not something that should be delegated early.

Beware these traps when making this assessment:

- The "It only takes me 5 minutes" trap. Perhaps, but unless you spend an hour or two teaching someone else to do it it will still be taking you five minutes every time in months and years to come. Also, other people may often be waiting for you to complete this 5-minute task.
- The "I like to do this task, so I know what is going on" trap. Invoicing or sales proposals typically feature here. You will still know what is going on if you devise appropriate processes, management reports and exception handling.
- The "It is too complicated to explain" trap. Complicated equals fragile, risky, inconsistent and non-scalable. It has

probably just evolved that way so now is your chance to simplify it.

USING YOUR DELEGATION PLAN

Once you have your prioritised plan, identify who should be doing each task – either because existing job descriptions and reporting lines define this or, in the absence of those things, because you believe someone will do a good job and the task should naturally fall within their remit.

Assess through discussions with them whether the person you have chosen is able and willing to take it on. Barriers might be:

- They are already too busy. This is not usually a problem if they see the new responsibility as interesting or adding to their influence.
- They don't have the experience or knowledge necessary. This means coaching them and perhaps investing in training.
- They want more money for taking on extra responsibility. This should be a fruitful conversation as if they succeed, they will be worth more to you (your freed-up time should be worth more than their time). Enhanced reward can then be linked to results.
- There is no-one suitable. If this is really the case (and not just an assumption based on existing roles and knowledge) then you have a recruitment need. This clearly needs to tie in with your business plan which presumably will predict increased net profit based on growth through delegation.

You need to create the process documentation unless this exists already. Ideally the new owner should create the process as part of the training and handover from you. You will also need to identify how results will be measured. This is critical as it is accountability for results that you are delegating, not just a task.

Finally, you need to identify a target date for handing responsibility over and a list of actions (for example, write the process down) that need to be carried out before then.

Once you have completed your Delegation Plan you should share it with the people concerned and review progress against it regularly.

> ### *Who Should Be Doing This?*
>
> *Many years ago, I was being appraised by my boss.*
>
> *He was the highly-successful Managing Director of an organisation that was crushing its targets. Ex-army, he arrived at 9am each morning and left at 5pm. In common with the rest of the Board and most managers through the business I was working silly hours – twelve-hour days from 7.30 each morning.*
>
> *At some point during the appraisal the conversation turned to delegation. My boss said "Nick, if I ever find myself actually doing anything, I look around to see who should be doing it." Those words stuck with me.*
>
> *Each time you start a new task, or look at your ever-expanding to-do list, ask yourself "Who should be doing this?" and then do something about it.*

CHAPTER NINE: YOUR ORGANISATION CHART

OVERVIEW

In this section you will create your Organisation Chart.

Your Organisation Chart defines a structure for your business. This is important because:

- Employees need to know where they and others fit in an organisation. Lack of clarity can be confusing and de-motivating.
- Growing and changing the business requires clear reporting lines and responsibilities.
- The process of formalising an appropriate structure will force you to address inconsistencies, gaps and duplications – and to consider how effective your people and processes really are.

- Defining structure leads naturally to defining outputs and so helps accountability.

Start by communicating what you are planning to do and why to your staff. Make sure this is two-way communication (find a way to get them all to contribute and listen to the results).

You are going to create your "to-be" structure first.

"TO-BE" STRUCTURE

It is easiest to start with the structure that you think you will need when you reach your vision, say in three to five years' time. This should be an ideal structure (that is, ideal to operate your future business), uncluttered by any of the existing anomalies, gaps and compromises.

There are some basic principles that you need to embody in your structure:

- Unity of command – every employee should report to one and only supervisor. (Do not confuse reporting lines with providing a shared service; for instance an administrator can support several managers but should only report to one person for pay and rations issues). Avoid dotted-line reporting lines.
- Each post should have clear responsibility for outputs or results matched with appropriate authority over the resources necessary to achieve this.

- Lean organisation – keep the total number of levels including the leader and the front line to a minimum – in most SMEs this will be between two and four
- Too many layers means excess information processing, long, slow decision making, people by-passing the structure, managers or even complete layers adding little or no value, feelings of disconnectedness both upwards and downwards and higher costs.
- Using a maximum span of control of seven means that organisations employing between eight and fifty people should aim for three layers. Four layers gets you to three hundred and fifty employees!
- Start at the second level with three main responsibilities reporting to the MD/CEO (see diagram below):
  o Get new business
  o Deliver the product or service
  o Get paid and balance the books
- There should be one position responsible for each of these roles (but this may not be three separate people in a small business).
- Do not design a structure to cope with or work around individual inadequacies or historical accidents – deal with them.

Use the example structure given in Figure 18 as the start point for your structure, adjusting as required. It will probably look quite different in the middle section but similar in the two outside sections. Try not to bring existing employees and job titles into it at this stage – you are developing the ideal structure to run your future business. Create the structure you will have at the point when you achieve your vision as set out above.

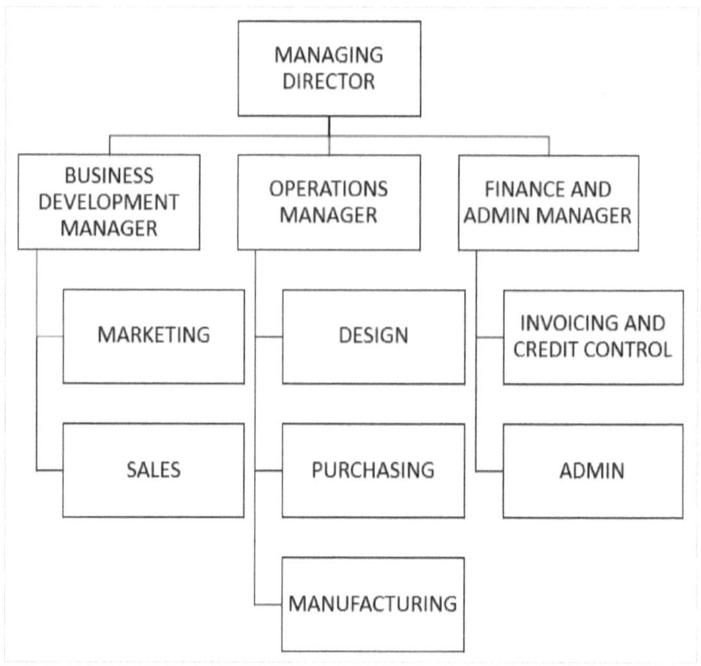

Figure 18 - A Generic Structure

Notes:

- The second level breakdown is generically get business – deliver service – get paid and this can be applied to any business.
- The layout from left to right, top to bottom, follows the natural flow of business through the organisation and so helps with process and KPI definition.
- In small businesses individuals may cover many roles (boxes) on this diagram - or perhaps there are things that no-one currently does. It is still useful to separate them functionally as shown.

- The "deliver service" third level will be very different depending on industry – this example is for a manufacturer.

ACCOUNTABILITY LIST

The Accountability List (Figure 19) asks you to think about all the major processes in your business and decide who is responsible for each.

You may not do all these things in your business but for each function you do have, check that each process is covered (will be done by) a position on your to-be Organisation Chart. Adjust the to-be chart accordingly.

Next, identify who is currently accountable for the results of each process and how results are measured. You are going to use that in the next section.

Process	Owner
Business direction and strategy	
Business plan and budget	
Marketing	
Sales	
Design	
Purchasing	
Manufacture or build	
Shipping	
Installation and/or service delivery	
Invoicing	
Collecting cash	
Management information	

Figure 19 – Accountability List

"AS-IS" STRUCTURE

Now bring it back to today and draw your "as-is" structure. You may already have an up-to-date Organisation Chart, in which case I suggest you just check it against the notes below and update it if necessary.

If you don't have an existing Organisation Chart, create one using the generic format from Figure 18 to get you started. Include actual job titles and the name of the incumbent. It will probably have fewer boxes than the "to-be" version and the same names may appear more than once.

Check the names on the diagram against the current process owners from the Accountability List and adjust the Organisation Chart as necessary. Grouping accountabilities by owner should help you put names into the boxes on the as-is structure.

Refer back to the guidelines above to make sure your as-is structure is fit for purpose. Some issues that are likely to arise are:

- Everyone in the business reports to you, even though you have managers and supervisors in place. This is your opportunity to start to address this by creating a structure and delegating responsibility for staff to the people concerned.
- Unclear or joint reporting lines; someone works for two or more people. It is usual for people to provide a service to different people – an admin assistant may support Sales and Finance, for instance – but they should only report to one person for "pay and rations" (and development and coaching and so on). Only the latter relationship appears on the Organisation Chart, which defines accountabilities, not processes or working relationships.
- Shared responsibility; two people each believe they are in charge of the same task or function. A variation on this is

where someone carries a title but doesn't actually do the work – someone else does. *This arises because you haven't made the difficult decisions and had the difficult conversations required to make it the sole responsibility of the best-suited person. Now is your chance.*

- Orphan functions; no-one appears to be responsible for something. Identify the best person to be responsible and add it to their responsibilities. Follow the advice in the chapters on Delegation and Job Descriptions.

- Someone carries out multiple functions – some sales and some operational stuff, say. This is pretty normal in small businesses. Decide whether this combination of responsibilities is valuable for the business by looking at the to-be chart – does the combined role exist when you are not constrained by today's reality? If not, separate the roles on the as-is chart and put the incumbent's name in both.

You may have some gaps where no-one is or could be responsible - put "Vacant" in those boxes – this tells you that will need to recruit or develop someone into the role.

APPLYING THE ORGANISATION CHART

Once you are happy with your as-is structure it is time to communicate this to all employees individually. Start with the most senior people and work down. Approach this exercise with a positive attitude but be prepared for some difficult conversations:

- Employees may see the existing lack of structure as being "flexible" or "responsive" in that at different times different people are apparently in charge of any given process. In fact, this situation means that whilst everyone may feel able to lend a hand when required, no-one is responsible for the results. Making responsibility clear should not prevent people being flexible and responsive.

- There may be roles where more than one person considers themselves to be in charge, meaning that you must make a decision and explain why.
- It may not be immediately obvious who should fill a role – you might not have the right person.
- Employees will understand this as a step towards performance management and may not be particularly happy about the prospect.
- As with all these changes, this is an opportunity to engage with your staff in a two-way conversation (that means ask what they think and listen to the answers).

Once you have told everyone, publish the as-is Organisation Chart so that everyone has access to it.

You may want to share the to-be Organisation Chart with certain key people at this stage – for instance the people who you see playing a bigger role in the growing organisation.

Boundaries Make You Free

My client, the new Managing Director of a specialist PR firm, had sent me some documentation in advance of a strategy workshop I was running for them.

Unfortunately, it seemed as if one of the files was corrupted; when I printed off the organisation chart the boxes with job titles were there, but the connecting reporting lines were missing.

I mentioned this to the MD in our brief meeting before the workshop and asked him if perhaps someone could print me a copy complete with lines. He seemed surprised. "Oh, we don't have reporting lines. We think that would make us inflexible and unresponsive to customer requests."

One of the issues that emerged in the workshop was that staff below the Board lacked innovation and never took responsibility or made decisions for themselves. I suggested that clearly defined accountability, authority and reporting lines meant staff could innovate and take responsibility within the areas that belonged to them. Conversely, they were unlikely to take ownership of problems if it was not clear that it was their problem, or if they did not know, metaphorically speaking, where the edge was.

The follow-up discussion about addressing this revealed the (pretty common) fact that one reason for leaving the structure hazy was that it avoided the need for some rigorous analysis, difficult conversations and hard decisions.

The fault was not in the employees but in the leadership.

CHAPTER TEN: YOUR EMPLOYEE JOB DESCRIPTIONS

OVERVIEW

In this section you will create your Employee Job Descriptions.

A job description describes why a role exists. It sets out the main few responsibilities of the role and how these are measured. Creating and agreeing a job description is a process of two-way communication about what is important and what success looks like.

This is an essential precursor to being able to manage performance and increase employee accountability.

JOB DESCRIPTION TEMPLATE

As usual, let your employees know what you are planning to do and why. Start with your direct reports so that they don't find out at the same time as their staff. Make the communication two-way by asking for their opinions and questions.

You should use your organisation structure to implement change from now on. This means that each manager or supervisor should carry this project out for their direct reports and so on down. Don't be tempted to short-circuit this by doing it all yourself but agree job descriptions for your direct reports first and then coach and support them to do the same for the next layer down. This is an investment of your time in developing their abilities and your business.

Give everyone who reports direct to you a copy of the sample job description shown in Figure 20. Give them a blank version of the template at the same time and ask them to have a go at completing it over the next few days. When you do this, schedule a time with each person to discuss their job description. Complete your own version of their job description before the meeting.

Job title	Service Manager		Reports to	Managing Director
Purpose of role	To provide support and maintenance to customers in accordance with their contract			
Main responsibilities			How measured	
Respond to customer machine faults within applicable SLA			% response within SLA as defined in report x	
Carry out planned maintenance on all customers' machines in accordance with manufacturer's standards			% late pms as defined in report y	
Maintain accreditation with suppliers x and y			Audit reports Training records per report z	
Ensure all work is carried out following Company HSE Policy			Audit report Training records per report z	
5.				
6.				
Key challenges	Rapidly changing technology – impact on training/knowledge			
Knowledge, skills, experience and qualifications	Level n qualified in supplier x and y equipment			
	Supervisory skills equivalent to ILM level 7			
	Field engineering experience			

Signed (employee):_________________________   Date: _______________

Figure 20 - Example Job Description

Keep the following guidelines in mind as you complete each job description:

- You are creating the ideal description of the role required by the business in this document. If someone is not doing it all, or not doing it all *well*, at present don't create a job description that matches what they can do now. You expect there to be a gap between each role and the incumbent's current performance - this drives their development and business improvement.
- Purpose = a single short sentence that gives the reason you employ them.
- Responsibilities method 1. Identify the thing you would ask them about if you had only 30 seconds to check their

performance. Then the thing you would ask about of you had 5 minutes, then 30 minutes. These are the top three responsibilities.

- Responsibilities method 2. Use the as-is Organisation Chart flow (left to right) to identify what is produced by each box (role) and where that output goes to. These outputs and inputs should give you a good insight into the responsibilities of the roles concerned. For instance, a Design Manager will produce manufacturing drawings but may also provide prices to Sales – this might indicate two responsibilities.
- Don't put something in as a measurement if you are unable to measure it! (You'd be surprised – or perhaps you wouldn't). The acid test is either it will be an unambiguous binary outcome (for example, "Yes, we were compliant") or you are able to look at the report that provides the measurement while agreeing the job description.
- Key challenges (if any) – the unusual or difficult aspects of the role that might require a special person to overcome them. You'll want to focus on these when recruiting for the role. Don't just repeat the responsibilities here and don't fill it with platitudes or standard challenges such as "Remaining calm under pressure" (unless you are recruiting an astronaut, say).
- Skills and knowledge – only the essential, provable capabilities should appear here – the things that, being absent, would disqualify a candidate. I still (2018) see "computer literacy" trotted out to fill a bit of space...don't put that in.

AGREEING JOB DESCRIPTIONS

Review the resulting job description with each employee, comparing it with the version they have produced. The wording will be different, but the scope should be more or less the same. Agree the final version, remembering the things to avoid:

- Trying to turn every possible activity of the role into a responsibility. Restrict it to the few critical responsibilities. Your contracts of employment should contain words to the effect that employees will do anything reasonable requested by management which will cover the rest.
- Trying to write your Operating Manual into a job description. Leave out detail and leave out how things are done.
- Using vague, generic or indirect wording ("Liaise with", "Review", "Set direction for"). Be direct and to the point using ordinary English ("Hit sales target", "Meet budgeted production volume").
- Not including measurement, or not being precise as to how things will be measured.

Where you have more than one person in a role (for example, many field service engineers) you only need one job description, which will apply to all the incumbents. In these cases, you should still endeavor to involve all of them in defining their job description and then consolidate and rationalise the results.

If you have distinctly different levels of experience and performance in a role you may want to have separate job descriptions (for example "Field Service Engineer" and "Senior Field Service Engineer"). The acid test is whether you can specify real emergent or higher-level responsibilities in the senior role. The advantage of grades is the career development path it gives; the disadvantage is complexity.

Once you have agreed the job description, have a neat version produced and both sign it. A copy should go on the relevant personnel file and the employee should get a copy.

Every role on the Organisation Chart should now have a job description.

> ### *Are These Any Good?*
>
> *The two guys running the business were driven and capable – but also stuck because they had to do everything themselves.*
>
> *They were trying to do things differently and had produced some job descriptions. At our first meeting they asked: "Are these any good?"*
>
> *In traditional consultant style I asked them a question in return: "What is the point of a job description?" After a brief discussion we decided that the point of job descriptions is the same as the point of a vision statement, or a strategy, or objectives. To communicate something. In this case, to communicate the reason the role exists and how success will be measured.*
>
> *If the effectiveness of a communication is measured by the change it brings about then many job descriptions are completely ineffective. Hardly surprising when:*
>
> *- They run to several pages and are stuffed with platitudes and standard phrases;*
>
> *- There is no simple statement of why the role exists;*
>
> *- Responsibilities large and small are jumbled together in no apparent order as if the writer wanted to record every minor task the role might possibly be involved with;*

- Details of how and when to do things clutter the job description instead of being confined to the Operating Manual;

- No clear means of measuring these responsibilities are given, whilst uninformative but faintly ominous words like "key", "critical", "timely" and "high quality" litter the document;

- They appear to have been created by someone who was in two minds as to whether they were writing a job description or an advertisement for a job vacancy.

The thing is, creating a useful job description (one that explains what is important and can be understood and remembered by a seven-year-old or a tabloid reader) takes much more time and thought than just...creating a job description. Like marketing or strategy, nine-tenths of the task lies in thinking and one-tenth in writing. Too often this ratio appears to have been reversed.

CHAPTER ELEVEN: YOUR EMPLOYEE OBJECTIVES

OVERVIEW

In this section you are going to set objectives for your key employees.

You have already set your strategic objectives and KPI targets - these are essential to achieving your business aims. However, they only come to pass when employees are given individual accountability for them. Without this step they remain as words on a flipchart or in your One-Page Strategy - stuck permanently in the future. Setting employee objectives for the next 12 months starts to make things happen.

Employee objectives also allow you to communicate what is required of an employee and measure whether it has been achieved. They usually form part of a performance management system, being set and reviewed annually.

Clear, achievable objectives provide purpose, context and a sense of achievement for the employee.

> *NOTE: At the risk of repeating myself, I again suggest you review the section "Plan the Change" in the "Successful Systemisation" chapter before embarking on any of the changes in this chapter.*

SETTING EMPLOYEE OBJECTIVES

Get your direct reports together and explain the purpose of objectives and the benefits for the business. Explain the logic that improved business performance will lead to improved career prospects and rewards for employees. Go through the example objectives sheet (Figure 21) together. Explain that each person should have a limited number of objectives which should include quantified targets for at least the most important responsibilities on their job description.

Employee Name	Fred Bloggs	Manager name	Jane Doe
Objective		Target	Review comments
Response to callouts		95% within SLA	
Carry out planned maintenance activities on schedule		99% complete within 20 working days of scheduled date	
Ensure the Company retains supplier x accreditation		Zero failures above level 2	
Ensure that all HSE audits for the Service Department are passed		Zero findings rated "concern" or above	
Implement the mobile call dispatch system by dd/mm/yyyy		Project complete and accepted	

Set date: ___________ Signed (employee): ____________ Signed (manager): _______________

Reviewed date: __________ Signed (employee): ____________ Signed (manager): _______________

Figure 21 – Example Objectives Sheet

Don't at this stage mention linking performance to reward or pay. If the topic is raised, then make it clear that achievement (or not) of objectives will have no impact on pay or other rewards until they have been in place for at least a year and everyone is happy that they are understood and fair. Once they are happy with the approach then, over time, objectives will be introduced for every role and may be linked to incentivisation.

Ask them to go away and draft their own objectives; you will also be drafting a set for each of them. Diarise individual meetings to finalise and agree them. Use the template in Figure 21 for this. Each person's job description should already be in place and define measurable responsibilities so turning these into objectives is simply a matter of setting a reasonable target for each for the next 12 months.

A good start-point for "reasonable" is what is being achieved now. That means you and the employee must be able to measure and agree this; you must be able to look at a report that provides this information before you agree the target. (It is completely pointless to set targets without having an agreed way of measuring them.) If you then want to stretch that target you must have some practical justification for this; that is, things that can be changed to improve performance. A ten-percent improvement with no visible means of support is neither fair nor compelling. Keep the following clear in your mind, particularly at the follow-up meeting where you agree objectives:

- At this stage your purpose is to introduce a change in culture and in the way your business is managed – not to create a perfect set of objectives that match your KPIs and business strategy and deliver a step-change in performance overnight.
- Your job descriptions are based on the ideal for the role. Unless you are very lucky most incumbents will fall short of this so imposing a perfect set of targets on day one would be unrealistic.
- You are asking people to take increased responsibility (even if the actual tasks remain largely unchanged). They need to grow into their redefined role and develop a sense of mastery and confidence. This is particularly true where you are asking them to formally manage others where this has been informal or unclear before. It needs to be understood by both of you that you are setting targets in order to agree what success looks like, not as a stick to beat people with.
- Objectives will change every year so over time you can add to and stretch them – that is performance management.

Some employees may ask what is in this for them – a reasonable question in the circumstances. It is also a positive sign that they recognise that they are being asked to take more responsibility and that they see the linkage between their results and those of the business. You should, however, avoid the temptation to put any kind of incentive or bonus scheme in place at this point because neither party can yet be confident about results. As a far-sighted and fair employer, you will want to share the benefits of growth with your staff when these materialise and some words to this effect will generally suffice at this stage. Obviously, if someone is changing role, or taking on significantly more work, then remuneration must be adjusted accordingly.

Having agreed objectives make sure that the Date Set is completed and signed by both parties. A handwritten version created in the meeting is fine – scan it and put a copy in the personnel files and give a copy to the employee.

REVIEWING PERFORMANCE

You should review performance against objectives annually as part of setting new objectives for the following year. This review should use the same form with review comments added to the last column.

Set aside sufficient time to do the review and agree new objectives (at least an hour, preferably two) and make sure it is in both your diaries well in advance of the day - in fact, there is nothing stopping you scheduling this meeting twelve months beforehand on the day you set the objectives.

Ask the employee to assess their own performance and make notes ahead of the review. Do the same yourself - it will severely undermine confidence in the process, the attention given to objectives and belief in your concern for employee development if you are ill-prepared or the meeting is rushed.

Your review should be based on evidence - if you have set unambiguous targets (see above) this should be straightforward. You may incorporate mitigation in the review comments if, for instance, a target has been missed due to circumstances outside the employee's control.

> *Note: If you are using objectives to decide on bonuses or some other reward then you may want to make it a little more quantified, with a weighting for each objective and a percentage for completion. However, as with everything else in the book, this is about communication and good communication is usually kept simple.*

Those objectives that are also measurements on the KPI Sheet will be reviewed monthly (see Monthly Management Review below). However, you should hold a brief performance review with each of your direct reports at least quarterly. This gives you both a chance to take corrective action and it emphasises that these targets are real, and this change is important. It would be pretty ineffectual management to let someone miss targets and drift off-line for 12 months before surprising them with a bad review. If someone is under-performing, then agree and document corrective action in the interim review meeting.

Set, Review, Repeat

My client, a software reseller, was familiar with creating KPIs; he had done it a couple of times already in his business. His problem, he told me, was that he was reluctant to go through the process with his staff again. We talked about this and it emerged that he was worried that his credibility when it came to such initiatives had been damaged by previous failures.

I asked why it had failed before and a couple of things became apparent. Firstly, previous KPIs had not all been clearly assigned to individuals and secondly, those that had been were not reviewed on a regular basis. In a matter of months, the KPIs had fallen into disuse.

It is not enough to create KPIs. It is not enough to assign them as someone's objective. They only take hold and start to be useful when people own them, and that only happens when regular performance reviews with meaningful conversations and consequences take place with the individuals concerned.

CHAPTER TWELVE: YOUR BUDGET

OVERVIEW

In this section you are going to create your Budget.

In systemisation, the budget is the heart of the business plan rather than an appendix to a long, wordy document. These numbers turn your strategy into financial targets which in turn are used to create non-financial targets such as marketing or operations KPIs.

These targets form the objectives for your staff and so link their daily activities to the vision for the business. Accountability and performance management are based on these targets.

Your Budget will cover the first twelve months month by month and then years two and three with a simple annual total. The key numbers from your budget (turnover, gross profit, net profit and cash balance) will also appear on your KPI Sheet.

As with all the products of systemisation your Budget is primarily about communication. In this case you are thinking through what you would like to happen over the next 12 months, expressing this in numbers and then validating (or sanity-checking) the result by looking at the things that need to happen to bring this about (and of course involving the people concerned in this process).

We add words to the plan only where they are necessary to explain the figures or capture some change, initiative or project that the plan requires.

The 10-Minute Business Plan (Figure 22) is a graphical view of the process described in this section.

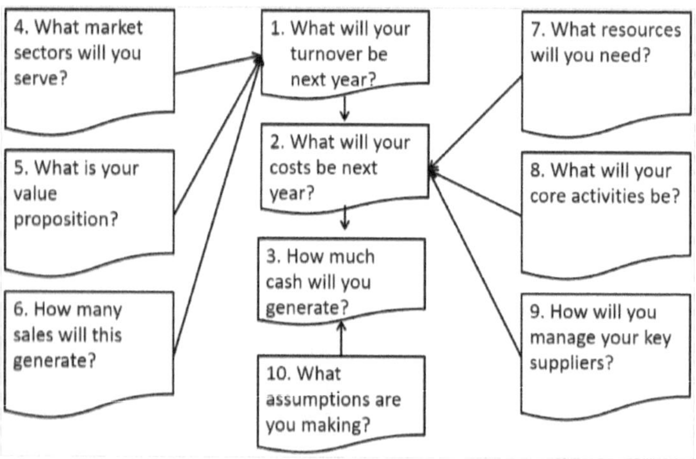

Figure 22 - The 10-Minute Business Plan

CREATING YOUR BUDGET

The easiest way to create a budget is to use a spreadsheet. Take the previous 12 months' actual profit and loss figures (often referred to as just "actuals") as the start point. The previous year's actual figures can generally be downloaded from your accounting system to a spreadsheet.

Before we go any further, a word on your profit and loss report:

Your Profit and Loss Report

The Profit and Loss Report (known as "The P&L") is one of the three main financial tools for managing your business. It shows the operating performance of your business in terms of how much you sell and how much profit (or loss) you make. The same layout is used for budgeted (future) and actual (past) performance. The report usually displays figures for a month, a year, or year to date (YTD). The report is more useful as a management tool if it provides comparisons, for example actual performance against budget or against the same period in the previous year. It is also more useful if it shows a range of periods, typically 12 months, so that trends are visible and single-month variability eliminated. It is also usual to show the key figures such as gross and net profit as % of turnover; changes in these ratios can be informative.

The table shows the main elements of a profit and loss statement; most businesses will have a more detailed breakdown of income and expenses in their P&L; that is, they will have more categories. It is entirely up to you how detailed this is - the overall structure will however be the same. (Note: figures are always shown net of any pass-through purchase tax such as VAT).

Figure 23 gives an explanatory layout.

Turnover	£ 1,000	aka Sales or Revenue. The total value of goods or services invoiced in the period. Neither your accountant nor the tax man care how you run your business so a single line will do for them. However, you might want to split income into sub-categories to help you manage performance against your strategy. For instance, Project Income and Recurring Income, or Product A income and Product B income. Ask your accountant to set up separate nominals (codes) to achieve this.
Less: Direct Costs		aka Cost of Goods Sold (COGS) or Variable Costs. The total costs invoiced in the month that are incurred directly and only as a result of sales. If you split income as suggested above, then you should slit direct cost in the same way.
Materials	£ 400	*The cost of any materials in what was sold e.g. steel in a car, apples in a supermarket*
Direct labour	£ 200	*The cost of any labour incurred directly and only as a result of sales. This means sub-contractors and staff paid only for productive hours*
Gross Profit	£ 400	Turnover minus Direct Costs
Gross Margin	40%	***This is a key performance indicator – gross profit/turnover***
Less: Indirect Costs		aka Overheads or Fixed Costs. Costs that are incurred whatever the level of sales.
Salaries	£ 200	
Building & accomodation costs	£ 50	
Depreciation	£ 10	*This figure is subtracted from the Fixed Assets line of the balance sheet*
Trading Profit	£ 140	aka Operating Profit or Profit Before Interest and Tax (PBIT). In many small businesses this will simply be called "Net Profit"
Trading Margin	14%	***This is a key performance indicator. In many small businesses it will simply be called "Net Margin"***
Interest	£ 5	
Tax	£ 28	
Net Profit	£ 107	aka Profit After Tax (PAT) or Retained Profit. This is what is added to the Retained Profit line of the balance sheet and is then available to pay dividends.
Net Margin	11%	

Figure 23 - Profit and Loss Report

The P&L is a powerful tool for understanding what is going on in your business

- The turnover and turnover split shows how well your strategy, marketing and sales are working.
- The direct costs show how well you are managing your suppliers and how efficiently you are using labour and materials.
- The indirect costs show how well you are managing central costs such as staff and buildings.

You should review the P&L every month.

FORECASTING

It is sensible to create your Budget using the same chart of accounts layout as your accounts package; that is, the same income and cost line descriptions in the same order. This will make it easier to compare actual figures with your budgeted figures as you use the plan to run the business. It will also make it easier to upload the budget to your accounts system if you want to do this.

Figure 24 gives an example layout.

The number you are working towards is the total net profit you require for the year however it is easiest to start with revenue (also known as income or turnover or sales). You can extrapolate from previous results or work this out based on number of sales and average order value, whichever you find easiest. Most business owners would want this to be more than in the previous year, but this is not a given. Whether revenue is budgeted to rise, stay the same or fall this line will require a sentence or two of explanation in the narrative. Boxes 4, 5 and 6 of Figure 22 suggest a way you might reason about and explain this forecast.

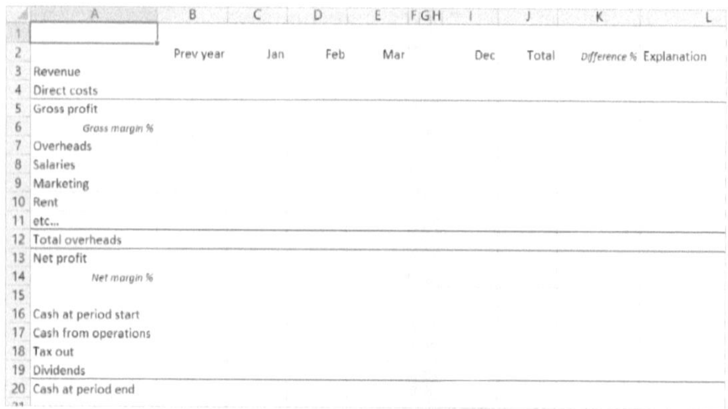

Figure 24 - Example Budget Layout

If you plan to extrapolate from the previous year, then download the last twelve months of actual figures to a spreadsheet. Now you need to decide what turnover level you are going to use to forecast the turnover line of your Budget for the next twelve months and then apply your known, anticipated or desired changes to these baseline figures.

If the business has changed significantly over the year, then take the last quarter's turnover figure and multiply it by 4 rather than the last 12 months – or if things have changed more dramatically you could even take the last months' figure (known as the run-rate) and multiply it by 12.

> NOTE: If you are a start-up and you don't have any previous years' figures then you will have to estimate your revenue based on your predicted number of sales and average order value. Costs can then be estimated by listing all the expenses you can think of.

Next work out your direct costs (also known as variable costs or cost of sales). These are the costs you only incur when you make a sale or provide a service. Usually they are split between labour (the cost of the time to provide the sold item or service) and materials (the cost of the item you have sold on, or of the raw materials you used to make it). In some businesses (such as manufacturing) these costs are relatively high whilst in others (such as consultancy) they may be very low. Note that labour costs do not include salaries but only variable costs such as subcontractors or employees who are only paid for the hours they work. It is usual to simply take the historical cost ratio (that is, direct costs as a proportion of turnover) and apply this to the revenue you have already planned. Again, any significant deviation from this ratio will require a sentence or two of narrative to explain why.

Your gross margin (the difference between income and direct cost, expressed as a percentage) will usually remain constant from one year to the next. If you are budgeting for a changed gross margin, then you should explain why in a sentence or two.

Overheads (also known as fixed or indirect costs) are those costs that are not dependent in the short-term upon the level of sales, such as salaries or rent. Again, the simplest way to budget these is to take the previous year's figures (or the last quarter's or the current run-rate as appropriate) and roll them forward before applying any planned changes. Again, provide a brief commentary on any significant changes. Figure 22, boxes 7, 8 and 9, suggest how you might think about your forecast direct costs and overheads.

This gives you your net profit figure. If this is not what you require then you can alter any, or all, of the revenue, direct or indirect costs. In this case you must note in your brief narrative for the lines(s) concerned what you are going to do to make these changes happen – for instance perhaps you are going to implement a new software package to make some function more productive.

Finally, you need to create a cash flow forecast for the year. This starts with cash in the bank on day one and then has the income from the business added to it each month. From that you must subtract known cash outflows, such as corporation tax, sales tax and dividends. Your aims must be a) to have no less cash at the end of the year (after you have taken out your own drawings from the business) and b) not to have a negative cash figure in any month on the plan.

> *NOTE: Your cash flows in will often be delayed; most businesses must wait to be paid for invoiced income. When you prepare your cash flow forecast make sure you take this delay into account, particularly if you are forecasting strong growth.*

When you are happy with your Budget you can upload it to your accounts system and copy the key lines to your KPI Sheet (see the relevant chapter below). You should also ensure that change initiatives identified in your narrative are reflected in individual employee objectives, the relevant plan (for instance, the Marketing Plan) or KPIs as appropriate. Otherwise they will never get beyond words on a page.

USING YOUR BUDGET

The headline figures of your Budget (turnover, gross profit, marketing costs, employment costs and net profit) will appear on your KPI Sheet and be reviewed in your Monthly Management Review (see the relevant chapter below).

However, it is important that you and your managers develop a good understanding of management accounts; finance is the language of business and you all need to be building a shared understanding of the business using that language. For that reason, I recommend that you review your P&L, Balance Sheet and Cash Flow Statement with your managers each month.

Your P&L should be reviewed against budget - if you have uploaded the budget to your accounts package then it will provide comparison reports.

You may be wary of sharing too much information with your employees - for instance, salary, net profit and dividend figures can all be sensitive. Using a simplified view of the figures, prepared in a spreadsheet, can avoid awkward conversations and misunderstandings.

You will identify strategic actions, projects or initiatives during systemisation. In this section we talked about the brief narrative that is required where a value in your Budget is forecast to deviate materially from previous periods. These two things should be aligned; if your narrative explains a change by referring to some business initiative or project then that should be on someone's objectives and reviewed under the "Projects" item on the Monthly Management Review agenda.

Somewhere Over the Rainbow

...budgets really do come true.

A common pushback when I suggest to a business owner that having a budget would be a pretty neat idea is along the lines of "...but they are never right" or, perhaps more poignantly "It won't make any difference to what happens".

The Managing Director of a mobile servicing company took this view. His business was successful and growing and he had never felt the need to go beyond a cursory glance at the annual accounts and checking the monthly bank statement.

I suggested that he should have, and use, a 12-month budget and cash flow forecast. He was not convinced.

A couple of months later he found himself in a cash squeeze caused by a quiet month and having to replace a couple of vehicles. He became more open to having a plan and we put one together. Two months further down the line a major customer gave notice. With the help of the plan he was able to predict the impact and take the necessary steps – including obtaining bridging finance from his bank.

Earlier in the book I suggested that the first and most fundamental change you need to make is one of mindset. Management is essentially about predicting, and so changing, the future. It is about bending the world to your will.

The absence of a plan is a confession to your employees and yourself that you cannot control the future and that results are in the lap of the gods. Having a plan and budget does not of course guarantee it will come to pass but it does mean you remain in control whatever happens.

CHAPTER THIRTEEN: YOUR SALES PLAN

OVERVIEW

In this section you are going to create your Sales Plan.

The Sales Plan takes your revenue (or income) budget and translates it into sales targets. This then provides a way of planning and managing your sales and marketing activities.

It defines your sales process from enquiry to sale together with the ratios and lead-times across each stage. It also sets out how you manage existing accounts to maximise revenue from them.

In this way it defines your sales KPIs such as average order value and sales pipeline value.

SALES PIPELINE

Before you start to enter data into the Sales Plan you will need to define your sales stages, if you have not already done this. Work through the Sales Pipeline Exercise (Figure 25) to understand (or refresh your memory about) the stages in your sales funnel. Use historical data to complete the numbers and ratios.

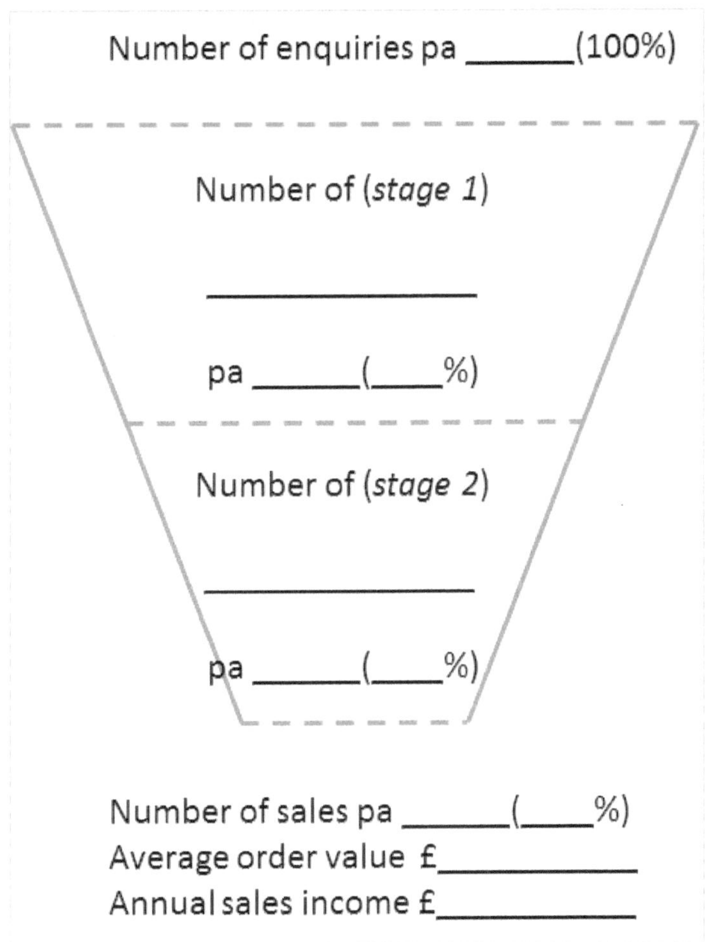

Figure 25 – Sales Pipeline Exercise

Use these stages to create your Sales Plan. The example in Figure 25 leaves you to define the names of each stage – if in doubt use the simple (but common) process which is simply New Enquiry -> Quoted -> Won/Lost. Some businesses might have an additional stage: New Enquiry -> Qualified Opportunity -> Quoted -> Won/Lost and some (for instance in financial services) may be much more complex. Use your own internal terminology (for instance "Lead" instead of "Enquiry" or "Proposal" instead of "Quote".

> *Note: Make sure that you have unambiguous definitions of these terms for your business. What constitutes an enquiry? What information is required and what checks must it pass?*

SALES PLAN LAYOUT

Figure 26 shows a typical layout for a Sales Plan (which you can also use for a sales report - you should use the same layout for your Sales Plan and your actual sales figures). You can create separate sheets or tables for each salesperson using a similar layout – this will allow you to manage individual performance.

If you are using a customer relationship management (CRM) system or sales system that produces this sort of report for you then use that – you will probably still have to create a Sales Plan separately though.

	A	B	C	D	E	F	G	H	I
1									
2		Jan	Feb	Mar				Dec	Total
3	New enquiries	6							
4	New quotes	4							
5	Closed walked	2							
6	Closed lost	2							
7	Closed won	4							
8									
9	Open quotes	9							
10	Quote bank value	£ 27,000							
11									
12	Won value	£ 11,000							
13	Conversion ratio	67%							

Figure 26 - Example Sales Plan Layout

You may want to create a single sales plan for your business (as we assume in this section) or, if you sell a range of distinct products or services, you can create one for each of them.

BUILD YOUR SALES PLAN

This section assumes that you are using a spreadsheet similar to Figure 26. It further assumes that you enter data into each cell; you can of course use formulas in your spreadsheet to remove the need to do this. If you are using a CRM for reporting, then make sure that your Sales Plan matches the CRM report layout as far as possible.

Having defined your sales pipeline stages, enter them down the left-hand column. Next set the plan dates (the months across the top) to match your business plan and budget timescale.

If you are an existing business, you probably already have open sales quotes (where quotes are created in one period but not closed until a later period) so you'll need to enter the anticipated balances in the first column for Open Quotes and Quote Book Value.

Now enter the monthly sales figures in "Won value" line for the 12 months. This value should match the revenue line on your business plan less any non-sales revenue such as contracted income. If you have split your Sales Plan between different products or salespeople, then the combined total should match your business plan.

> *Note: Not all your salespeople will hit target. It is usual for the combined targets to exceed the budget figure to allow for this.*

In the Pipeline Exercise you calculated your average order value (AOV). This allows you to calculate the number of orders required in the "Closed won" line; that is how many average value sales you need each month to achieve the Won value line.

From the data in the same exercise you know how many enquiries you need for each sale you win so you can complete the New enquiries and Sales lost lines, where Sales lost equals the difference between New enquiries and Sales won.

> *Note: If you are starting your business then you will have to guess this – three losses for each win would be a conservative ratio to start with.*

You can leave the "Closed – walked" line at zero for now. This is for you to record where you decline to pursue an opportunity – maybe the prospect fails your credit checks, or the solution required is too complex and risky, or just not what you do. If there are too many of these it indicates that your marketing is missing the mark at least some of the time.

You now have a complete Sales Plan with a matching set of sales KPIs. Average Order Value, conversion rate and required number of new enquiries are particularly useful as these numbers can be improved by altering your sales and marketing activities and skills. Quote bank value is a very useful indicator of future revenue.

ACCOUNT MANAGEMENT

For most businesses, it is easier (and cheaper) to sell more to existing customers than it is to go out and find new ones. Even though it is easier, it still requires a planned approach.

Before you create a Sales Plan for your existing customers, read these few words about cross-selling:

Cross-selling

There are two opportunities for cross-selling. Firstly, you can look for customers who only purchase some of your products but who you think purchase (from someone else) some of your other products. For instance, if Customer A buys printer cartridges from you but not printer paper you can be fairly sure they are buying paper from someone else.

A Customer/Product Matrix (sometimes called white space analysis) can highlight this - see Figure 27.

	Product A	Product B	Product C	Product D
Customer 1		Y		Y
Customer 2	Y	Y		
Customer 3			Y	Y

Figure 27 - Customer/Product Matrix

Where a customer has not yet bought one of your products then use this as the basis for a communication strategy for that customer. For instance, from the above analysis you could talk to Customer 3 about Product B. Don't assume that customers know about all your products – they may think of you only as a supplier of what they have already bought from you. This is a great reason to keep marketing to existing customers.

The second opportunity is where you have low penetration into a customer; you are only supplying part of their requirements for a product. You can establish this through market intelligence (your field engineers tell you that other manufacturers equipment is in use) or estimates (if a typical company in sector A purchases one new computer for every three employees every year and customer B is only buying one per six employees...maybe they are buying them from someone else).

Note: Canny procurement types will make sure that they don't end up relying on a single supplier and so may pursue a policy of limiting the proportion of their business they give to you. This means that all that lovely extra business you think you can win is not really there. It will avoid a lot of tantrums in sales reviews if this is established early on in the account planning process.

Use both these techniques to develop your sales targets for existing accounts. At this stage you might want to go back and adjust your revenue line and direct costs on your Budget.

Once you have your existing account sales target you can adapt the same sales planning spreadsheet template for existing accounts to plan and track the sales from to renewals, upgrades or additions.

Salespeople can have a mixed target (new sales plus existing accounts) or you can have separate new business sales and account development sales teams. The latter approach recognises the fact that new business sales and account management usually require different skill sets. If you have a single set of salespeople with a mixed target, then this can be addressed in the commission scheme.

COMMISSION SCHEME

The Value Won line is your sales target and can be divided up amongst your salespeople. If you want to use a commission scheme (most companies do) then you can now implement one.

Why do you need a sales commission scheme?

The underlying assumption is that rewarding salespeople financially for performance will encourage them to work harder and sell more in pursuit of those rewards. This view is partially borne out by academic research although some studies suggest commission works for simple, transactional sales but against more complex, relationship-based sales. In practice sales commission schemes are almost universally used. A carefully-designed commission scheme when implemented on top of good management practices, a compelling proposition, training, and a solid sales process is a useful management tool – but it is not a substitute for these things.

Here is a (rather long) list of things you should consider when implementing a commission scheme:

- Commission schemes are usually implemented at individual level, although team-based commissions may be used for large complex sales where a support team is necessary.

- Ensure that the rewards incentivise the behaviour you want. You may want different behaviours from a major account manager and a new business field sales representative.
- Think carefully about the balance between basic salary and commission. The two combined form the OTE (on-target earnings) and, since we are assuming commission influences behaviour, we must also assume that this balance will have an impact on the motivation and behaviour of the salesperson:
  o The lower the proportion of basic salary the higher the OTE, since you are transferring risk to the salesperson.
  o A high basic may mean that salespeople do not need any sales to achieve their minimum acceptable income.
  o A low basic may result in aggressive sales behaviours or high staff turnover.
- Decide whether the scheme should be based on sales revenue or gross profit:
  o Revenue is relatively easy to measure but may result in unwanted price discounting
  o Gross profit supports pricing and margins but is more difficult to measure and can be open to manipulation in complex sales.
- Think about possible behaviours and outcomes if salespeople have multiple ways to earn commission. Avoid situations where salespeople can achieve their target by focusing on what is easiest to sell – this may not be the balance of sales you are aiming at. Some scenarios where you have this are where targets are split between:
  o New customers and existing accounts
  o New sales, renewals and updates
  o New equipment and refurbished equipment
  o Credit deals or single payment
- Implement appropriate controls on the sales process, such as:
  o A pricing model or pricelist
  o Sign-offs

- o   Commission payments only after contracts are signed
- Understand that every commission scheme will have unwanted side-effects, such as:
  - o   If a salesperson feels they are not going to achieve target this period, they may hold back new opportunities to the next period
  - o   Individual targets will prevent salespeople working as a team or spending time on anything that does not contribute to their personal target
  - o   Salespeople will go after the easiest opportunities, which might not be the ones that matter most strategically or financially
- In many industries, long-run sales performance is achieved by thinking long-term. For instance, gathering data on current providers and when current providers' contracts expire will not help a salesperson hit this year's target – but a commission scheme that builds this process in will pay dividends in the long run.
- Check that you can afford all possible outcomes and that better performance against the commission scheme results in improved net margins for the business under all circumstances.
- Make sure that commission targets in total exceed the sales income budget – assume a conservative proportion of target sales will be achieved.
- The overall commission scheme rules should be published annually, and each salesperson should have a written copy of their own targets and rewards, signed by them and their manager, before the year starts.
- Review performance with each salesperson monthly.
- Keep it simple (easy for me to say, at the end of a three-page list of bullet-points).

Other Approaches

Sometimes a straightforward commission scheme is inappropriate or insufficient:

- For a newly-hired salesperson. In this case it is usual to agree a ramp-up period, perhaps with a zero target for a few months whilst the product and market is being learned. This period should coincide with the new employee's probation period.
- For a trainee. The ramp-up approach can also be used here. In addition, the salesperson's activity can be measured as an indicator of effort and future success. Typically, this would include number of calls made, number of new leads, number of appointments booked, pipeline value and so forth – the activities matching the organisation's sales process.
- Where individual sales are few, large and have a long sales-cycle. In these circumstances it is possible to pay some of the commission on deal development stages. To do this, stage achievement must be objective and provable; for instance, "Achieved approved supplier status" or "Proposal submitted". Clearly, this involves the risk of paying commission on deals that never happen. It is also complex to administer. Alternatively adopt a high basic/low commission structure that provides adequate income during the periods without deals but still rewards results in the periods where sales fall.
- Some companies operate a platinum club or similar, with expensive foreign holidays for top sales performers. This recognises that for many people in sales it is about success and recognition as much as the money.
- Nothing beats saying "Well done" to them in public. Sales people are human too.

Add your sales KPIs from the Sales Plan to your KPI sheet. You should also add the cost of your sales commission scheme to the direct costs section of your Budget.

CUSTOMER RELATIONSHIP MANAGEMENT SYSTEM

Sales is about moving an opportunity through a process that takes it from the first contact through to sale and beyond. A Customer Relationship Management system (CRM) will help you define, measure and manage this process.

A CRM system is a database that holds information about your customers, prospects, contacts, opportunities, marketing campaigns, sales, and sales activities. With most systems you can set the system up so that it matches your own sales process or product, that is; you add or rename fields so that you can hold the data that defines your sales pipeline.

A CRM system will increase your sales by:

- Helping you keep in regular contact with customers and prospects – reminding them of service anniversaries, informing them of new products and services
- Making sure you follow the sales process so that opportunities are followed-up and converted
- Helping you understand where leads and sales come from so that you can focus your marketing accordingly.

CRM systems used to be hugely expensive and complex but with the advent of cloud computing they are affordable for even the smallest business.

To implement a CRM, start by identifying the information you need to understand and communicate with your customer. This will usually be basic contact information plus data specific to your business (for example car registration for a garage, or number of rooms for a carpet fitter). You will also need a Source field against each opportunity - did it come from email marketing or networking? Include steps to gather this data in the above process.

Search online and select a system that can be set up to match these information needs and your sales process (the stages you identified earlier in this chapter). Other things to consider are the total number of records you will need to hold – many cloud systems are free for a small number of customer records, but you need to plan for growth. A more sophisticated consideration is the other cloud-based systems the CRM will link to – often an accounts system, an email marketing system, a timesheet system and so forth. Most systems will also offer a free evaluation period.

Once you have selected the system, load enough data to test that the system will do what you need.

Successful full implementation will require you to change the way you work in order to get the full benefits. Make sure your sales, service, marketing and admin processes are changed to gather and use the new information.

USING YOUR SALES PLAN

The Sales Plan will provide some key performance indicators (KPIs) for your KPI Sheet, typically total sales pipeline value (the sum of the estimated sales income from open opportunities at period end); income won, or gross profit won, in period; conversion rate (number of wins divided by number of wins plus losses). These KPIs will also be on someone's job description and objectives sheet - typically your Sales Manager. These figures will be reviewed every month at your Monthly Management Review (see below).

It is common to hold sales reviews weekly. These reviews will use the Sales Report format but will also look at each open opportunity to see how and when it can be closed. Sales activity (calls, sales meetings and so on) is also reviewed; there should be a strong element of coaching in the meeting.

The Sales Trap

My client had a common problem.

The business had grown because she is great at selling the product. However, she just couldn't hire anyone else who could do it as well. The trap goes something like this:

- First hire someone who has had "sales" in their title previously and typically has been working for a succession of local competitors
- Explain your product
- Give them a target, a car, a laptop, a logon to the CRM and a mobile phone
- Cross your fingers
- Get increasingly despondent over the next 6 months
- Fire them
- Repeat

Incredibly she had been through this six or seven times. I suggested to her that perhaps it wasn't the people being hired that were the problem...

After she had calmed down, I got the chance to explain that I didn't have a magic bullet. Hiring staff is difficult to get right. With salespeople it just becomes obvious that it's going wrong sooner, and in numbers.

However, hiring people into an organised process designed to deliver results (instead of into a mess) can move the odds of success in your favour. Here is a different approach:

> • *Analyse who and what succeeds in sales in your business*
> • *Be crystal-clear about your niche, problem and proposition*
> • *Define your selling process down to script and question level*
> • *Implement a sales management process supported by effective tools*
> • *Write a job description*
> • *Define an induction process that starts with your Marketing Story. When the recruit can explain this to you at the drop of a hat move on to product training and sales process coaching. Maintain regular one-to-ones*
> • *Set ramp-up targets*
> • *Follow a recruitment process that is designed to reject early and that selects on intelligence and drive*
> • *Take a long-term view*
>
> *If you have the time to grow your own, perhaps by identifying operational staff who get on well with customers and developing them, you are likely to get a better result.*

CHAPTER FOURTEEN: YOUR MARKETING PLAN

OVERVIEW

In this section you are going to create your Marketing Plan.

Your Marketing Plan is derived from your Sales Plan. It needs to deliver the volume and quality of enquiries or leads required to achieve the planned value of sales.

Without a plan, marketing can be haphazard and ineffective. It becomes difficult to track what marketing is being done and which marketing is working. Like everything in business, effective marketing requires a process and routine.

Your Marketing Plan describes what marketing activities are going to take place, how much time and money each will require and what results (enquiries, and eventually sales) you expect from them.

Your Marketing Plan defines your marketing KPIs, such as number of leads required per period and average cost per lead.

MARKETING AUDIT

Start by carrying out a marketing audit for your business using the template provided in Figure 28.

identify all your current marketing activities. The audit contains a non-exhaustive list of promotion techniques – you can adjust this to include ones you use if they are not shown.

Item	Don't use	Use but don't know if effective	Use and proven effective	Spend per year £	Resulting sales per year £	Resulting profit per year £	Return %
Print advertising							
Flyers/inserts							
Radio advertising							
Referrals/word of mouth							
Direct mail							
Yellow pages							
Online directories							
Online PPC/banners							
Own website & SEO							
Email marketing							
Social media							
Trade shows							
Networking							
Tender journal subscriptions							
Telemarketing/telesales							
PR							
Strategic partnerships							
Seminars/events							
Cold calling							
Catalogues							
Renewals and upgrades for existing clients							
Totals							

Figure 28 – Marketing Audit Exercise

If you are not sure what results you are getting in terms of cost and resulting sales, then use estimates.

> *Note: Your costs should come from your accounts system. Your marketing spend should be split into the different marketing methods you use so that you can track how much you spend on each one and so how effective they are. Ask your accountant to create nominal codes or analysis codes for each marketing method you employ (for instance, emailing, networking, trade shows). Your opportunity and sales results by marketing source should come from your CRM. Refer to the guidance on selecting a CRM in the previous section. If you are not able to produce these marketing performance figures, then either you don't have a CRM in place or it is set up wrongly. You need a CRM to manage marketing properly.*

After you have completed the audit you might decide to continue with the promotion methods you are currently using, or you might want to change or adjust them. Make sure you review current activities and collateral against your Marketing Story to check that they are appropriate; does your website need editing? Do you need to redo brochures or email copy? In this way you can be more confident that your marketing won't just deliver leads, but the right leads.

MARKETING PLANNER

Use the Marketing Planner (Figure 29) to create a marketing plan that will deliver the number of enquiries that are needed to meet your Sales Plan (the "new enquiries" row on the Sales Plan in the previous section) whilst taking into account the hours and budget available for marketing.

	A	B	C	D	E	F	G	H	I	J	K	L	M	N	O
1	Activity	Direct spend per year	Internal hours spent per year	Internal hourly rate	Total annual cost	Leads per year	Cost per lead	Conversion rate	Sales per year	Cost per sale	Average sale value	Gross margin	Profit per sale	Annual gross profit	Cost per £
2	Website + SEO	£ 3,000	60	£ 20.00	£4,200	180	£ 23	25%	45	£ 93	£3,000	40%	£1,200	£ 54,000	£0.08
3	PPC	£ 3,600	24	£ 20.00	£4,080	180	£ 23	25%	45	£ 91	£3,000	40%	£1,200	£ 54,000	£0.08
4					£ -		£ -		0	£-			£ -	£ -	£ -
5					£ -		£ -		0	£-			£ -	£ -	£ -
6					£ -		£ -		0	£-			£ -	£ -	£ -
7					£ -		£ -		0	£-			£ -	£ -	£ -
8					£ -		£ -		0	£-			£ -	£ -	£ -
9					£ -		£ -		0	£-			£ -	£ -	£ -
10					£ -		£ -		0	£-			£ -	£ -	£ -
11					£ -		£ -		0	£-			£ -	£ -	£ -
12					£ -		£ -		0	£-			£ -	£ -	£ -
13					£ -		£ -		0	£-			£ -	£ -	£ -
14					£ -		£ -		0	£-			£ -	£ -	£ -
15					£ -		£ -		0	£-			£ -	£ -	£ -
16					£ -		£ -		0	£-			£ -	£ -	£ -
17	Total	£ 6,600	84		£8,280	360	£ 23	25%	90	£ 92				£ 108,000	£0.08

Figure 29 – Example Marketing Planner

The Marketing Planner shows your expected return on investment from marketing overall and for each marketing activity. In the example shown the business plans to spend 8% (8p in every £) of gross profit on marketing in order to generate the planned amount of business.

Once you are happy with your Marketing Plan, adjust the marketing spend lines on your Budget to match the direct spend per year shown. Once again, we see how systemisation is an iterative process not a linear one.

As you track actual performance these figures will become more reliable and useful. Some businesses perfect a single marketing approach (the one that gives them the best return) and concentrate on that. You should be cautious about doing this; a mix of marketing methods spreads the risk, forces comparison and promotes learning and innovation. "One" is a dangerous number in business, whether it means one customer, one supplier, one marketing channel - or one key person.

MARKETING PROCESS

It is important that every marketing activity is focused on one thing: Generating leads. If you are not careful, marketing becomes an end in itself. This risk is increased when you hire someone to do marketing (who may be somewhat remote from the commercial imperatives of your business). It can also be increased by the prevalence of social media usage in modern marketing, where the goal can be displaced from "getting enquiries" to something like "generating connections". The latter is useful for most businesses as a marketing channel, but only a KPI if you are a teenager being paid by a make-up company to blog about lipstick to millions of other teenagers.

You should create a Marketing Process diagram, like the examples provided in Figures 30 and 31, for your own business.

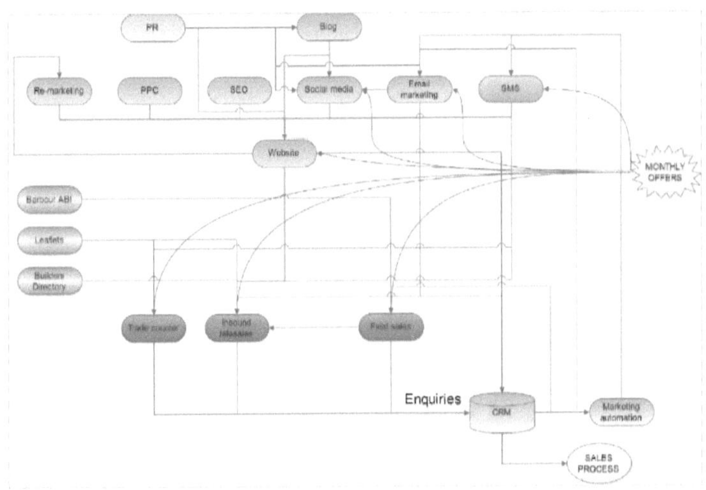

Figure 30 – Example Marketing Process – Wholesaler

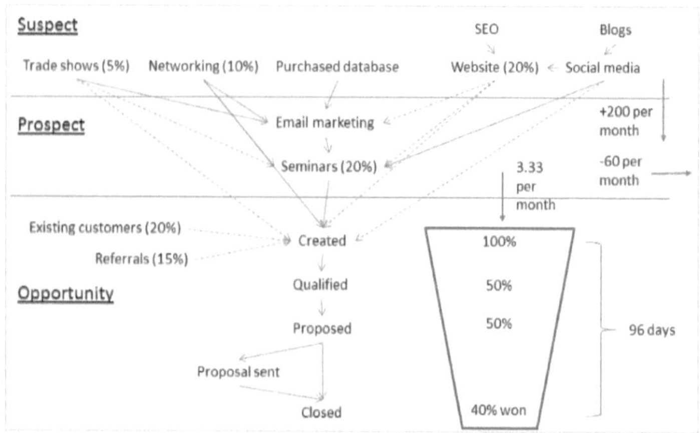

Figure 31 – Example Marketing Process – Professional Services

Your marketing process should make it explicit how every marketing activity is expected to lead to more enquiries. The acid test is that, whenever you ask them, your marketing person (or provider) should be able to explain exactly how their current activity results in more enquiries.

MARKETING ACTIVITY PLANNER

The next step is to create your Marketing Activity Planner. A suitable template is given in Figure 32. This sets out in detail what needs to happen and when.

Marketing Activity Planner				
Annually	Quarterly	Monthly	Weekly	Daily
Promotion				
Set marketing objectives and budget				
		Review enquiries generated v plan and budget		
		Send email newsletter		
	Update website			
			Publish blog	
				25 social media posts
Trade show x				
	Run seminars			
Proposition				
Review niche, proposition and competition, update marketing materials				

Figure 32 – Example Marketing Activity Planner

Complete this by transferring the activities and numbers from the Marketing Planner above.

Once you have completed this activity breakdown, check that the people concerned will have the time to carry out all the activities! It is not unusual for a business to create a great marketing plan that is completely impractical when it comes to the effort involved. In the above example, has anyone calculated how long it will take each day to create twenty-five social media posts? If the person responsible for this is already busy, what is going to stop so that this activity can take its place? In most businesses, this conversation does not take place, the owner blithely assumes a quart can be got into a pint pot - and the marketing doesn't happen.

If necessary, go back and adjust the promotion plan and budget again to arrive at an achievable activity plan.

USING YOUR MARKETING PLAN

Once you have agreed the detailed list of activities make sure that they are transferred to two places. First, make sure that each person concerned knows what they must do and when, and that this is in their work diary as a recurring task. Secondly, make sure that the owner of the marketing results (often your Marketing Manager or Marketing Co-ordinator) has those results in their objectives.

You will generally have two key marketing KPIs on your KPI Sheet; number of enquiries and cost per enquiry. This means they will be reviewed monthly in your Management Meeting. Either in that meeting or in a separate marketing meeting, performance against the Marketing Plan should be reviewed - how are your individual marketing activities performing in terms of enquiries generated and their cost?

Why Your Marketing Manager is Failing

The word "marketing" is universally used to describe a whole bundle of activities designed to generate business enquiries or leads. This generalisation is not useful when it comes to recruiting marketing staff or outsourcing marketing activities.

Traditional breakdowns of marketing focus on stages (awareness/interest/commitment)   or   the   mix (price/position/promotion) or the proposition (niche/pain/proposition). These are all useful models for developing your marketing but again are not particularly helpful when recruiting or outsourcing.

For example, a role titled "Marketing Manager" in a small business will often encompass a wide range of activities such as marketing strategy, planning, website maintenance, email creation, database list creation or purchase, social media content, tele sales, Google analytics, email stats, events – and so forth. Because funds and manpower are limited there is a tendency to bundle anything remotely marketing-related into the job description.

This wide range of activities (and so required skills) can often result in performance issues and even a general reaction that "marketing doesn't work". This can be damaging both to the business and the employee or supplier concerned.

It is more useful in these circumstances to think of marketing as being three different sets of skills:

Strategic (the development of the context and strategic goals for marketing). This requires a high degree of conceptual thinking, the ability to envision the long-term future, a deep understanding of the organisation's competitive strengths and weaknesses and business strategy. These tasks are best undertaken by the leadership team of the business, if necessary, supported by a suitable external consultant;

Professional creative (the development of compelling messages, content and copy and the selection and set-up of the necessary technology and tools). This requires creative flair, deep knowledge of the tools and techniques required and an instinct for words and images that can change what people believe. These tasks are best undertaken by a professional marketeer by outsourcing to a marketing agency or freelancer;

Planning, execution and analysis (the scheduling and delivering of marketing content, the operation of the necessary tools and technology and the analysis of marketing effectiveness). This requires an aptitude for organisation, routine, accuracy and numbers. Such people are often already within an organisation in administrative roles – the skills are not specialised.

Whilst someone employed to do all of these things will, in the right circumstances, improve their understanding and performance in the areas that are not their natural strengths, the talents required are so different that this improvement will be limited. In most small businesses where exemplars or even fellow-marketeers will be limited or non-existent the poor jack-of-all-trades is almost destined to fail. I suggest you employ a marketing administrator and outsource the other two levels.

CHAPTER FIFTEEN: YOUR SERVICE PLAN

OVERVIEW

In this section you are going to create your Service Plan.

Your Service Plan helps you understand what resources (people, machines, licenses or vehicles, for instance) will be required to deliver the planned revenue and to deliver the customer service set out in your One-Page Strategy and Marketing Story.

It defines how many resources you need and the assumptions you are making about KPIs such as productivity and utilisation to get to these figures. This in turn is used to identify changes to the way they are used or managed to improve profitability.

Your Service Plan also includes customer-facing KPIs, such as delivery time and error rates. All these KPIs will be added to your KPI Sheet.

SERVICE PLAN

Start by identifying the resources that you use to deliver your service – this could include, for instance, call-centre agents, field service engineers, workstations, lathes, vans, mortgage advisers – anything that forms a significant part of your cost and whose numbers can if necessary be adjusted over the life of your plan.

This would exclude, for instance, factories. Closing or opening a new factory would be a separate major financial decision. It would also exclude, as another example, a basic toolset for an engineer or a desk for a tele sales agent – these costs are one-off and relatively small.

The Example Service Plan shown as Figure 33 starts with the revenue line from your Budget. Let's suppose you provide IT support and plan to increase turnover from £180,000 per month in January to £220,000 per month in December. Let's further suppose that each technician can handle £100,000 per month in support (some maximum number of customer users). Somewhere between January and December you are going to have to take on a new technician (unless you can increase individual productivity somehow).

	A	B	C	D	E F G	H	I
1							
2		Jan	Feb	Mar		Dec	Total
3	Planned revenue	180000	185000	190000		220000	2400000
4							
5	*<Resource type 1>*						
6	Productivity revenue/resource/month	10000	10000	10000		10000	
7	Number required	2	2	2		3	
8	Cost/resource/month	30000	30000	30000		30000	
9	Total cost for resource type	60000	60000	60000		90000	
10							
11	*<Resource type 2>*						
12	Productivity revenue/resource/month						
13	Number required						
14	Cost/resource/month						
15							
16							
17							
18	Customer KPIs						
19	KPI 1	0.95	0.96	0.97		0.99	
20	KPI 2	5.5	5	5		4.5	

Figure 33 – Example Service Plan

You can see a couple of things from this plan. Firstly, the profit from your increased revenue is pretty severely dented by the cost of the extra technician. Secondly you now have capacity to service £300,000 of income so your profitability will come back as, or if, you continue to grow. Thirdly, if you could squeeze another 10% of productivity from your existing technicians you can delay recruitment and get growth as well as increased profit (although if you continue to grow then clearly at some point you will have to add resource).

Note: If yours is an existing business that has been trading already, then the obvious start point is to use the quantity of each resource that you have already. If it is a new business, then you will have to estimate how many you will need to achieve your planned revenue.

Productivity per resource (for instance income per field engineer or income per accountant) can be derived from historical data for your business. Sometimes there are industry benchmarks you can use for comparison or you may wish to arrive at your own targets.

If your Service Plan shows productivity improvements then you should add a brief narrative to your Business Plan, for instance "productivity improved by training x", or "productivity improved by increasing van stock".

You are trying to achieve your revenue plan with as few of each resource as possible whilst taking into account the risk associated with single points of failure or overstretched resources.

When thinking about the latter complete the final part of the sheet, customer KPIs. These need to measure the attributes you are competing on, identified as part of your Marketing Story and One-Page Strategy work. In this way you start to turn your strategy into action. Your resourcing plan needs to match this strategy. For instance, if your strategy and market positioning depend on a lengthy interaction and a relaxing experience for customers but you have pared the number of service reps to the bone then clearly there is a mismatch which will result in disappointment for customers and, eventually, shareholders.

In the example in Figure 33 the two customer KPIs might be system availability and average fix time. Note that they are planned to get better; this will need some intervention or change, especially if management at the same time decide to squeeze productivity. These interventions or changes must be assigned to someone, usually through their personal objectives, and their implementation monitored.

Note: Not all customer KPIs will appear here. For instance, if you are competing on product range and availability then this will be related to stock rather than service resources.

USING YOUR SERVICE PLAN

Once you have arrived at a balanced plan that you are happy with, make sure that the resource costs on your Budget are adjusted to match this. If you plan to increase (or decrease) resource levels make sure that any associated one-off costs are added to the business plan as well.

I mentioned a couple of KPIs; productivity (revenue or profit per service head) can be used by any business but your customer KPIs will be industry or business-specific. Whatever you select as service KPIs, add them to your KPI Sheet and review them during your Monthly Management Review.

If you have identified actions to improve service or productivity, then these will be in the objectives of individual employees and also in the business plan and should be reviewed accordingly.

> ### *Trust Your Instincts?*
>
> *My client is a mortgage broker. We had systemised much of his business and he had standard models for his mortgage advisors (target fees/month) and we were discussing the same approach for his mortgage administrators.*
>
> *Historically he had run with one administrator for every two mortgage advisors and this was his current level of manning. We had set up a system to track administrator productivity and had the results. Before we looked at the figures my client and his Admin Manager said they thought the people concerned would be all producing about the same but that they knew who would be best (a long-standing and cheerful employee) and worst (a relatively new and somewhat taciturn employee).*

In fact, in terms of mortgage value processed per period, the new employee was around twice as productive as the person my client thought would be best. Now, there were some extenuating circumstances, so the comparison was not absolutely accurate, but broadly my client was wrong. Furthermore, the figures suggested that it should be possible to significantly reduce the level of administrative time per mortgage if everyone came up to the level of the best.

Simple measurements can challenge assumptions and highlight dramatic improvement possibilities for your business.

CHAPTER SIXTEEN: YOUR OPERATING MANUAL

OVERVIEW

In this section you are going to create your Operating Manual.

Great businesses deliver consistently good results regardless of how busy they are. They deliver consistently good results regardless of who is on shift, or on holiday or sick. We have probably all visited a restaurant, had a great experience, recommended it to friends – and then on a subsequent visit endured poor service or cold food. That sort of swing in quality is the sign of an un-systemised business.

Consistently good results (for both internal customers and external, real, customers) require solid, repeatable processes that have been designed and honed to deliver the same outcome time after time. These processes are documented and used to train people so that your customers' experience is not dependent on the right chef being on duty, or the receptionist being in a good mood, or the programmer being experienced enough to fill in the gaps in the specification.

For all these reasons it is essential that all the key processes in the business are documented, publicised and accessible.

This section is about starting your Operating Manual, not finishing it (which never happens). Think of it instead as setting up a receptacle for organisational learning. Whenever a problem is solved and a better way of doing things emerges, this is where you record it for everyone to use when necessary in the future.

There are two possible approaches to creating an Operating Manual; you can attempt to document every process that goes on in your business in one go or you can start by just documenting solutions to problems that are causing you a headache today.

Just thinking about the first approach would make me feel a little tearful; the second approach is the one I suggest you take. The objectives for this section are therefore to set up your Operating Manual, to communicate the reasons for having such a thing to your employees and to get your first couple of processes documented.

WHAT FORMAT SHOULD YOU USE?

The first thing to do is to communicate your intention to your staff, which can be done at your next team meeting (if you don't hold monthly team meetings then now is a great time to start).

Note: If you hold team meetings or something similar and they are characterised by you doing all the talking whilst attendees gaze out of the window, look at their phones or scratch themselves then here is your chance to make these events more effective.

Rename them "Business Improvement Meetings" and run them in a way that all attendees are forced to get involved – the workshops described in previous chapters are a format you could adopt. Ask them to come up with and present a solution to a problem that you have chosen. Select the best and agree actions to implement it.

You can still include the things you communicate in team meetings now; latest business results, date of the Xmas party, marriage banns, whatever.

After you have explained the benefits of building an Operating Manual then he first thing you must decide in the meeting is the format for your Operating Manual. The most common and flexible format is a single word-processed document (see Figures 34 and 35).

Note: This example took several years to get to this stage. It started with a single section on the organisation's sales process!

5.3.3 Creating a Contact

Create a new CONTACT record by using Main menu/Contacts/New Contact or the large New button (when on the Contact screen) or the large New button, drop-down "Contact".

Fields you should always be able to complete are:

- Company (select from the drop-down menu. You should always create the COMPANY record before the CONTACT record. Do NOT just type in the Company name – Act will accept it but the CONTACT will not be linked to a COMPANY);
- Phone
- Mobile
- Email
- Full address
- At least one Activity under the Activities tab (see section on Creating an Activity);

Note 1: To save entering common data such as address multiple times, create the COMPANY record without any shared information, create and link the CONTACT records without any shared information then add the common data to the COMPANY record. When you save it, Act will ask whether you want to apply the changes to related Contacts.

Note 2: Contacts are defined as unique by their email address. The system will warn you if you are creating a contact with a duplicate email address - including a BLANK email field.

5.3.4 Removing a Contact

If a Contact leaves a Company then if there is any relevant CONTACT history (that is , other than system and audit messages) then this should be copied and pasted into the new CONTACT record with a note stating the previous Contact name and email address. The old CONTACT record can then be deleted.

Alternatively, the old CONTACT name and email can be updated to the new Contact details. Again, a note stating the previous Contact name and email address should be added.

Figure 34 – Example Operating Manual Content

Figure 35 – Example Operating Manual Structure

Sometimes organisations are more comfortable with a collection of individual documents in a shared folder. For this approach it helps to use a standard layout when describing a process (see Figure 36).

Reference:	4.1
Name:	Order Job Materials
Description:	Order materials for a specific job if they are not stocked items.
Owner:	Storekeeper
Trigger, frequency, volume:	New sales order. Up to 5 per day.
Inputs:	Parts list on sales order quote
Outputs:	Order record on accounts system. Order emailed to supplier. Delivery date recorded on manufacturing system.
Performance measurement:	Sales despatch on time in full (OTIF) % using report OTIF100 from MRP System.
System access required	MRP System
Detailed steps:	
1	Check report SO200 (unfilled parts on sales order)
2	Get pricing from two suppliers
3	Create purchase order using screen x on system y
4	
5	

Figure 36 – Example Process Definition

Other companies use a spreadsheet, which provides powerful filtering and manipulation of individual processes and may impose more discipline on process definition. An example of the spreadsheet approach is given in Figure 37.

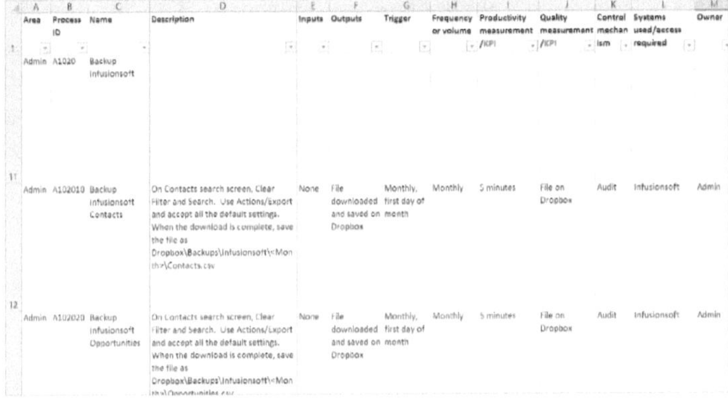

Area	Process ID	Name	Description	Inputs	Outputs	Trigger	Frequency or volume	Productivity measurement /KPI	Quality measurement /KPI	Control mechanism	Systems used/access required	Owner
Admin	A1020	Backup Infusionsoft										
Admin	A102010	Backup Infusionsoft Contacts	On Contacts search screen, Clear Filter and Search. Use Actions/Export and accept all the default settings. When the download is complete, save the file as Dropbox\Backups\Infusionsoft\<Month>\Contacts.csv	None	File downloaded and saved on Dropbox	Monthly, first day of month	Monthly	5 minutes	File on Dropbox	Audit	Infusionsoft	Admin
Admin	A102020	Backup Infusionsoft Opportunities	On Contacts search screen, Clear Filter and Search. Use Actions/Export and accept all the default settings. When the download is complete, save the file as Dropbox\Backups\Infusionsoft\<Month>\Opportunities.csv	None	File downloaded and saved on Dropbox	Monthly, first day of month	Monthly	5 minutes	File on Dropbox	Audit	Infusionsoft	Admin

Figure 37 – Example Operating Manual (Spreadsheet)

Some organisations use some form of wiki, or define tasks using functionality within an existing system such as the knowledgebase in a helpdesk system. It is also possible to use video which can be quick to create but time-consuming to change when processes change. Finally, you can buy specialist software for documenting business processes.

CHOOSING PROCESSES

Having agreed how you are going to record processes you can ask attendees to suggest which processes should be improved and documented first. You may want to structure this part of the discussion by preparing a couple of questions that help people identify problem processes; for instance, where things are frequently late, have an unacceptable level of defects or take lots of time and effort to do.

Having selected a couple of processes you need to identify the owners. This should be relatively straightforward as you have already implemented job descriptions and an Organisation Chart. However, processes almost always cross boundaries and indeed it is at these handoffs that problems often become apparent (and quality can be improved). In this case you will have more than one owner working together to implement the new improved process.

Here are a few words on improving processes:

Root Cause Analysis

Root cause analysis is a way of getting beyond the apparent cause of a problem and getting to the underlying, originating cause. This allows effective intervention to solve the problem rather than simply treating the symptoms. This analysis is best done in a group or brainstorming environment which is facilitated to ensure open-mindedness, participation and communication. It will not work in a culture of blame.

This diagram in Figure 38 can be used as a framework:

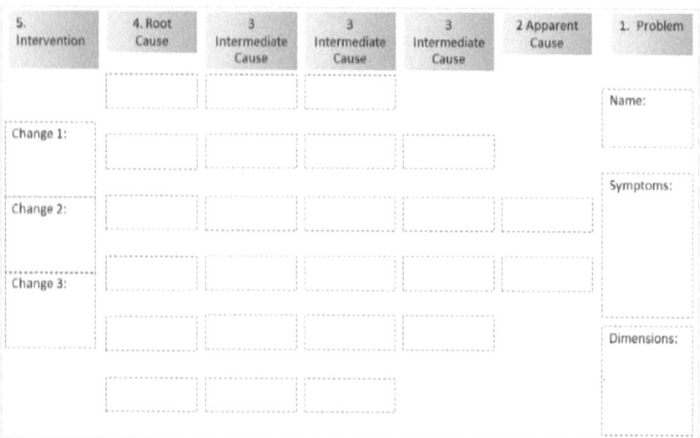

Figure 38 - Root Cause Analysis

The first step in solving a problem is to define it properly. Section One asks you to do this by completing the three boxes. "Dimensions" means how often does the problem occur, or how many times, or what proportion of outcomes are unacceptable or similar measures as appropriate to the problem. For example, "Twenty percent of materials deliveries arrive late, which is typically 10 per month".

Section Two asks you to identify obvious or immediate causes, for example "This is sometimes because they are ordered too late". Whilst this seems a good reason it doesn't really help you come up with a solution – so you need to keep going – perhaps "This is sometimes because the project procurement schedule is incomplete". In the diagram above this would go in a box in the right-hand intermediate cause column.

Another "Why" might produce the cause that "Because the drawings are accepted by production before the bill of materials is complete". This now sounds like something that could be changed through an intervention; a change of process around manufacturing drawing acceptance.

Note: In the chapter on Organisation Charts I mentioned that the outputs from one box or function form the inputs to another. You can think of your business as a series of flows. Earlier in this chapter I suggested that these hand-offs are a place where quality issues emerge and where interventions can make a big difference, quickly. This root cause analysis example seems ripe for a simple checklist solution; if the information is not complete it gets sent back. Atul Gawande explained in "The Checklist Manifesto" (Gawande, 2011) how checklists are a simple but effective way of improving outcomes.

The diagram allows for up to five "Whys?" – the so called Five-Whys model. You don't have to use them all.

The diagram allows for multiple causal chains – you don't have to use all of them, either, but real-world problems will often have multiple causes, so you should look for these.

USING YOUR OPERATING MANUAL

I suggested that you make your regular team meetings "Business Improvement Meetings". In between your Business Improvement Meetings, you need to support any process improvement work that is underway without removing ownership or accountability from the employees concerned. You may, for instance, need to provide guidance on root cause analysis. You may need to help them simplify rather than add more complexity. You may need to provide admin support to document the results.

Initially, your monthly Business Improvement Meetings will be the means by which you move your Operating Manual forward. At the same time, you need to take every opportunity to explain and demonstrate to staff that process improvement is everyone's job and it happens every day. Whenever something goes wrong you should ask the people involved about the cause and how they think the process could be improved to avoid a repetition – then get them to document the better way.

There are other triggers for documenting things in your Operating Manual. We have already covered delegation, and how the process you (or anyone else) is delegating needs to be documented and tested.   Recruitment is another event that requires solid, documented processes to be in place if you want a successful outcome.

Because developing a useful Operating Manual is a long-term process of developing a culture of continuous improvement, it will take consistent, steady leadership from you. If and when you are tempted to skimp on this, stiffen your resolve by reminding yourself that as well as a better business today, solid, documented processes mean a better selling price when you exit - so every addition and improvement to the Operating Manual means a richer you one day.

> ### *The Power of Small Changes*
>
> *Successfully implementing an Operating Manual often comes about through making small, local changes and then documenting them rather than documenting large, far-reaching ones and then trying to get people to follow them.*
>
> *The MD of a distribution business was concerned at the level of incorrect items that were being shipped. The change he made was for the warehouse person who picked the order to sign the picking list as correct and the van driver who loaded the order to sign it as well. This small change significantly reduced shipping errors, presumably due to a mixture of increased traceability and clearer accountability.*
>
> *The same business had a problem with warehouse operatives being under utilised during parts of the day, especially while the Warehouse Manager was not around. Creating a monthly, weekly, daily routine task schedule with task descriptions and checklists meant that everyone was able to be productive throughout the day even when there were no goods to be processed in or out.*
>
> *Both these changes went into the shared folder on the network that is the company's Operating Manual. More*

> *importantly both changes demonstrated to the people concerned that they could and should be looking for ways to improve things.*

CHAPTER SEVENTEEN: YOUR KPI SHEET

OVERVIEW

In this section you are going to create your KPI Sheet. You have already identified some key performance indicators in the preceding chapters and this is where you bring them together and review the complete set.

Identifying the correct KPIs will allow you to monitor the performance and direction of your business quickly and without having to get involved in the actual processes being monitored. If you think about your car you control that with a few dials on the dashboard yet there are thousands of things going on and being measured that you know nothing about. Think of your KPI Sheet as the dashboard for your business, showing the targets for the next 12 months and the actuals for the last 12 months.

Typically, your KPIs will include numbers tracking marketing, sales, customer service and financial results.

I recommend that you start this with a workshop with your key staff using the KPI Workshop Agenda shown here. However, once again, it is perfectly possible to work through the agenda by yourself.

KPI Workshop Agenda

1) Introductions (if necessary)
2) Objective (To identify the key performance indicators that are most relevant to your strategy)
3) Exercise - Strategic Objectives
4) Exercise - Goal Hierarchy
5) Exercise - Choose Your KPIs
6) Summary and close - next steps (Select or create the required reports to track the selected KPIs; Revisit job descriptions and objectives to agree who is responsible for each KPI and what a good target would be; Add the selected KPIs to the KPI Sheet; Revisit the One-Page Strategy in the light of the selected KPIs).

ONE-PAGE STRATEGY

Start with a review of your One-Page Strategy, particularly the basis on which you compete and the critical changes you have identified. For each of these try to identify the ways in which you might measure progress – these are candidate KPIs.

Use brainstorming and a flip-chart to generate and capture the ideas. If you start by handing everyone a post-it pad and ask them a specific question, perhaps "Looking at our One-Page Strategy, how many things can you think of that we might want to measure to see how we are doing?" then this will help your delicate plants to contribute and restrict the amount of air-time consumed by the more self-confident.

Looking back at Figure 15 (the example One-Page Strategy given earlier) we can see turnover, net margin, percent turnover from online sales and percent turnover from channel partners all get a mention. At this point these would all become candidate KPIs, but the brainstorming should produce a lot more at a lower level.

Use the flip-chart to identify and group common themes - these will indicate more candidate KPIs.

GOAL HIERARCHY

The Goal Hierarchy exercise is a way of organising your candidate KPIs - it will also generate some new ones.

Your top-level, strategic, objectives will be achieved by making things happen lower down in the business and so this exercise asks you to drill down to those things. For instance, a top-level objective of increased net profit of x is fine, but it doesn't tell you what changes need to be made. You need to turn it into more actionable measurements such as, say, increase average order value to y.

Breaking strategic goals down in this way not only allows you to change performance but also allows you to measure things that are drivers of your desired outcomes. These tell you what is going on sooner, and in a way that is closer to your actions. Both these facts make these KPIs more useful for your day-to-day operational decisions.

The example company in Figure 39 is a field service business. Their target of "Revenue resilience" refers to increasing the proportion of contracted revenue - this is predictable and, in the short term, locked-in – so a Good Thing.

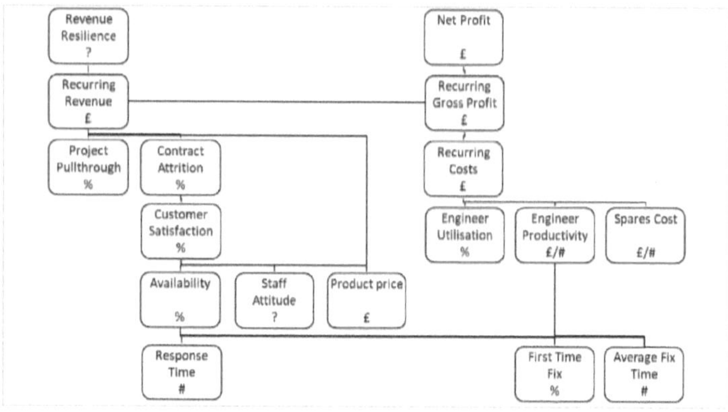

Figure 39 - Goal Hierarchy

You can see that this organisation developed two lines of thought; one focused on adding and retaining support contracts by improving service quality and one focused on direct costs by looking at repair time and costs. These each generated some sensible KPIs, some of which linked to both strategic goals. Note that it would be quite possible to generate a completely different hierarchy from the same start point - perhaps one focused on sales and sold margin. The point, once again, is communication; you and your staff are developing a shared mental model of the business and its workings.

Looking back at Figure 15, that example organisation might have turnover and net profit at the top and then "Online sales" and "Channel sales" on the second row. Presumably, their niche focus delivers superior margins so "Average premium" and "Retention rate" or something along those lines might appear.

To run this exercise, give everyone a copy of Figure 39 and talk them through the process. Give each person or group a blank flip-chart and ask them to pick one of the KPIs from the previous exercise. Make sure they choose one that is relatively strategic (that is, a top-level outcome for the business) not something that is clearly lower-down. Ask them to create their own hierarchy.

When they have done that, conduct a show-and-tell session.

CHOOSE YOUR KPIS

You should now have lots of flip-charts with a lot of candidate KPIs.

Not all KPIs are equally useful. In this exercise you are going to identify six to eight that are right for your business.

Useful KPIs have the following attributes:

- They are an outcome (for example, number of leads) rather than a driver (for example, marketing spend).
- They measure the effectiveness of some action you are taking to change the business.
- They are easy to measure (ideally already on a report but if not, already in a system that can produce a report).
- They tell employees what is important.
- They avoid encouraging obvious unwanted behaviours.
- They relate to your strategy (they fit a goal hierarchy that links KPI to business results). The acid test is: Could an observer deduce your strategy from your KPIs?

The Choosing KPIs Exercise in Figure 40 helps you evaluate each KPI against these attributes. Hand this out to each person and ask them to rate each of the KPIs that they think should be on your dashboard.

Indicator:				
Is an outcome (eg sales revenue rather than number of sales meetings)				
Is close to, and can measure the impact of, a strategic intervention (eg new sales opportunities rather than invoiced gross profit)				
Is easy to measure (ie you already record this, or it won't involve lots of additional work to do so)				
Sends a clear message (eg on time and budget, rather than happy customer)				
Avoids unwanted behaviour (eg speed of response ignores speed of fix)				

Figure 40 – Choosing KPIs Exercise

In the show-and-tell session that follows ask people to put forward their top-rated KPIs, justifying their choice. As you capture this on a summary flip-chart you should be getting close to a set of KPIs that are a good fit for your business and your strategy.

USING YOUR KPI SHEET

Make sure you keep all the flip-charts from the workshop! Work through the results and select your final six to eight KPIs, adding them to your KPI Sheet. You should have already made a start on this sheet using your headline financial figures (see the Budget chapter above). Figure 41 shows a simple KPI Sheet layout with some example KPIs (yours will be different of course).

	A	B	C	D	E
1					
2	TARGETS	Jan-18	Feb-18	Mar-18	Apr-18
3	New orders				
4	Average order value				
5					
6	Turnover				
7	Gross profit				
8	*Gross margin*				
9	Net profit				
10	*Net margin*				
11					
12	Average delivery time				
13	Returns				
14					

Figure 41 – Example KPI Sheet

You can track actual results against target by copying the plan sheet and using it to track actuals. This then provides a dashboard for your business that you can use as the basis for your Monthly Management Meeting.

You should try to present KPIs and all other management information in a consistent format so that employees get familiar with it. Here is a brief note on using management information:

Using Management Information

What is Management Information?

- Management information is the KPIs that form the dashboard for your business plus the more detailed supporting reports. It is reviewed monthly at your management meeting.
- It includes a full set of financial reports (profit and loss, balance sheet and cash flow statement) as well as key performance indicators.
- It is designed to help you navigate longer-term, wider or underlying strategic issues as well as control current performance.
- It does this by allowing you to see ratios, trends, deviations, changes or anomalies.
- To do this, management information is trended, compared with budget or history or displayed as ratios. It may sometimes help to generate insights if it is displayed graphically as in Figure 42. However, beware mistaking lots of fancy graphs for good management information; the acid test is "How has this data helped us improve the business? If it hasn't, why are we spending time on it?".

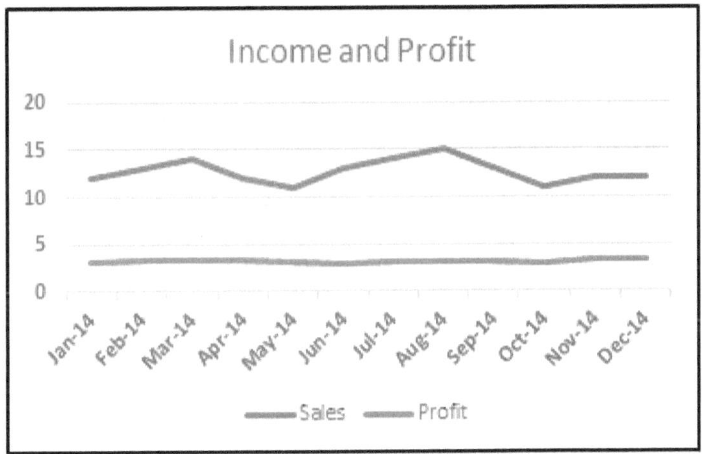

Figure 42 – Example Summary Management Information

Why is more information less useful?

- Masses of detailed information is not useful when you are trying to steer the business.
- It is difficult to assess sales trends by examining page after page of sales reports – but very easy given a simple graph of sales over time.
- Detailed information should be used to drill into, and answer, questions posed by management information. For instance, the lines in Figure 40 might prompt the question "Why does our gross margin vary so much from month to month?" To answer this question you might want to look at a more detailed sales report (see Figure 43).

Sales			
	Name	Value	Profit
Sale 1	Smith	£ 10,000	40%
Sale 2	Jones	£ 2,000	30%
Sale 3	Bloggs	£ 4,000	20%
Sale 4	Finney	£ 3,500	25%
Sale 5	Lofthouse	£ 12,000	60%
Sale 6	Matthews	£ 8,400	23%
Sale 7	Charlton	£ 2,500	46%

Figure 43 - Example Detailed Management Information

The value of management information does not lie in the numbers – it lies in the questions it prompts, the conversation that follows and the actions that are taken.

Now you have added the KPI row headings to the sheet but what about the actual target values? We talked about agreeing these under Employee Objectives and about setting some of them as part of creating your Budget, Sales Plan, Marketing Plan and Service Plan. Again, systemisation is an iterative process: You should revisit these items and make sure things are still aligned.

Once you have done this your KPI Sheet will be a sound basis for developing accountability in your employees whilst achieving your business plan. The KPI Sheet forms the basis of performance management in your Monthly Management Meeting, described in the next chapter.

Regular review, discussion and adjustment drives home the importance of these targets and makes them relevant for employees.

> ### *What Gets Measured*
>
> *I worked with the management team at a communications equipment reseller. Unsurprisingly, delivery lead-time and returns (sending the wrong thing) were both identified as KPIs.*
>
> *Returns due to picking errors had been a problem in the company for some time, persisting despite my client's efforts to introduce quality checks and processes to address it. Introducing this as a KPI had progressed things from a growing sense of unease to a measurable problem.*
>
> *They decided to display returns performance on a coloured chart in the office, over the desk of the administrator responsible. Each day this person would have to mark with a pen the number of wrong item returns received.*
>
> *Within a couple of weeks, the number of returns plummeted. Crystal clear ownership of a simple metric and highly visible tracking of results did the trick.*

CHAPTER EIGHTEEN: MONTHLY MANAGEMENT REVIEW

OVERVIEW

In this chapter you will set up your Monthly Management Reviews.

The Monthly Management Review serves three purposes: It is where you and your management team control the performance and direction of the business; it is where you develop the management team and it is where you develop the individuals on the team.

The meeting is based around the KPI Sheet, which is your shared model of how the business works.

This meeting provides regular, immediate review and feedback to you and your team about how well you are delivering the business plan. It is pointless to create a twelve-month plan and then not look at it until eleven months have passed (don't laugh, it happens). The meeting also completes the accountability loop for you and your team; knowing that your performance will be reviewed each month concentrates minds!

MONTHLY MANAGEMENT REVIEW

The Monthly Management Review is a critical element of a systemised business. It should become the central part of your management routine, the drumbeat that sets the tempo for your business.

The Monthly Management Review is the means to develop accountability in your direct reports (whether or not they have the title "manager"). Every month you discuss performance against their KPIs and targets. Without this regular review these will be forgotten and will play no part in driving business performance or teaching your employees that you expect them to take ownership of their results.

The first task is to decide who should attend this meeting. The start point should be your direct reports as shown on the Organisation Chart. You might exclude from this any admin staff who report direct to you – your PA for example.

Next, create an agenda for these meetings along the lines of the example given below. Initially you might want to simplify this but make sure every attendee has a slot where they report on the performance of their part of the business.

Example Agenda for Monthly Management Review

1) Review actions from previous meeting
2) Marketing report
    a) KPIs – performance v target
    b) Marketing activities v plan
    c) Market and competitor update
3) Sales report
    a) Sales KPIs - performance v target
4) Finance report
    a) Profit and loss
    b) Working capital
    c) Cash flow statement
    d) Aged debtors
    e) Cash flow forecast
5) Operations report
    a) Operations KPIs – performance v target
6) Staff matters
7) Projects update
8) AOB
9) Date of next meeting

Now make sure that you have the necessary management information to use in the meeting. The heart of the Monthly Management Review should be the KPI Sheet, but you should have the source reports available as well just in case (revisit the section "Using Management Information" above). When you agreed objectives with your direct reports you will have also identified the reports to be used.

The Monthly Management Review should be scheduled to take place at the same time each month and you should protect this time and ensure that the meeting is held without fail. The first time you allow the meeting to be cancelled or allow someone to miss it because they are doing something "more important" will spell the end of its credibility for attendees. Make sure that meetings are continuously scheduled 12 months ahead and in all attendees' diaries. Figure 42, "Monthly Management Cycle" gives a view of this process.

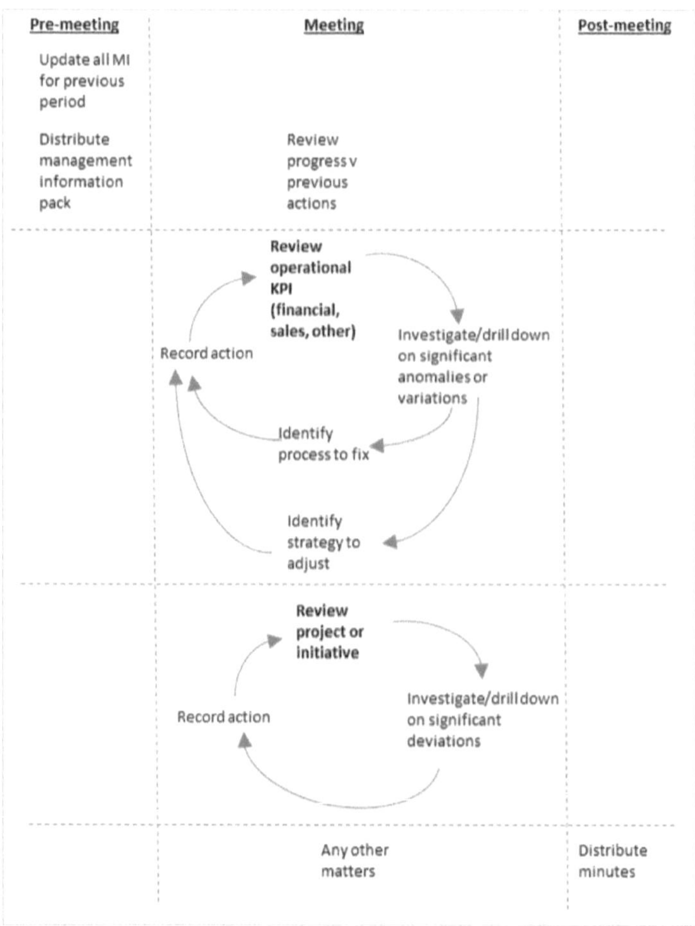

Figure 44 - Monthly Management Cycle

In the first meeting you should explain what you are trying to achieve and how you want the meeting to work; what it is for, what the outcome of each meeting needs to look like, how meetings will run, how you expect attendees to contribute and behave.

Leadership guru John Adair (Adair, 1988) talks about developing managers by working on three levels:

- The task - you manage the performance of the business against the plan.
- The team - you develop yourself and your managers into a high-performing team.
- The individual - you develop the managerial and commercial capabilities of each team member.

You need to stay aware of these three imperatives as you run the meetings. The first happens naturally. The second can be raised by you at the end of meetings either routinely or as and when examples of good or bad team performance present themselves. The third can be dealt with in mini-coaching chats with individuals after the meeting or in your regular 121s with them. Make sure that you take a few minutes to take notes and reflect on these two areas after each meeting.

MANAGEMENT TEAMS

If you want to continue to grow your business, you need to develop an effective management team:

- As SMEs grow it becomes more difficult for the founder(s) to run the business on their own – they need to find ways to involve other people in defining business vision and strategy.
- Delegation means managing through objectives and key performance indicators (KPIs) and this requires both a shared

vision and a management forum to review performance and decide actions.

- You will almost always arrive at better decisions when you discuss them and arrive at a joint view.
- Often potential acquirers put a high value on the quality and performance of the management team – after all, you won't be there anymore.

The management team:

- Creates the organisation's vision
- Defines the most effective strategy to achieve this
- Sets priorities for resources and actions (the plan)
- Reviews performance against plan
- Decides and assigns actions to keep the organisation on track.

Members of effective management teams:

- Think in terms of the whole organisation first and their own function second
- Move easily between detail (tactical) and overview (strategic) perspectives
- Have a shared conceptual model of the business and its strategy
- Accept responsibility for overall organisational performance and expect challenge from others on their own functional areas
- Display empathy for their colleagues' points of view.

Patrick Lencioni, in his book "The Five Dysfunctions of a Team" (Lencioni, 2005) suggests that high-performance teams demonstrate individual accountability based on:

- Commitment to the goals of the team gained through
- Challenge and constructive conflict enabled by
- Trust between members.

Using some of the ideas from "Senior Leadership Teams" by Ruth Wageman, Debra A. Nunes, James A. Burruss and J. Richard Hackman (Wageman, Nunes, Burruss, & Hackman, 2008) you can start to develop your management team by taking the following steps (see Figure 45):

- Make explicit the purpose and functioning of the Management Team and the responsibilities of its members (that is, the central circle).
- Design the process so that the purpose is supported (for instance by the necessary management information) and development of an effective team becomes an explicit activity.
- Manage the membership. Where necessary change the team performance of individual members by providing training, feedback and coaching. In SMEs this may be problematic:
  - o The senior management layer may consist largely of supervisor-level staff who have little or no management experience and may also consider that they didn't sign up to run the business but to carry out a functional role
  - o You are probably the main shareholder and the person accustomed to making all the decisions and so may not naturally draw out or encourage other's input.
- Change the membership. This is usually the MD's direct reports by default so poor performance in the Management Team may have wider ramifications for the future growth of your business.
- Set clear norms for behaviour, for example letting other people finish what they are saying, empathising with others' feelings, arriving on time, being prepared, not wasting time on small stuff, speaking with one voice outside the meeting and so on.
- Be aware of your leadership behaviour. Nothing in this chapter is advocating democracy or abdication of responsibility for the final decision but effective leaders

change their leadership style to suit the circumstances and develop other leaders, not more followers.

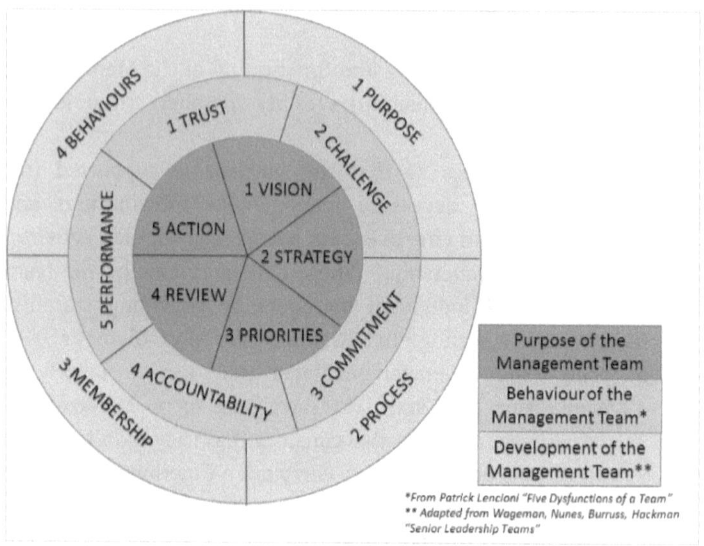

Figure 45 - Developing Your Management Team

RUNNING YOUR MANAGEMENT MEETINGS

Effective meetings take practice. Over time you will get better at running them and your team members will get better at contributing to them. Here are some closing guidelines to get you off on the right foot:

1) Always start on time - make late arrival unacceptable.

2) Always circulate all reports (see Using Management Information in the previous chapter) at least one day before the meeting. It helps to have someone organised who prepares and circulates them.

3) Expect people to have prepared properly for the meeting by having read all the reports (including their own – yes, really).

4) Limit the time and finish when that time is up. Decide how long you are going to spend on each agenda item. Appoint a timekeeper.

5) Stay focused – if the conversation gets into detail or off the point call time on it and suggest the relevant people take it offline. This meeting is a commercial review of business performance and how to improve it, not an operational meeting.

> *Note: I may be being unfair, but it is often the case that the person who does most of the talking (and not always to any great relevance, purpose or effect) is the business owner. If this gross generalisation applies to you, check the habit. Set an example and make sure that everyone else is brief and to the point.*

6) Stick to the agenda.

7) Appoint someone to record and circulate actions – who, what, by when - within one working day of the meeting. Don't circulate anything else.

8) At the end of the meeting check that everything you spent time on and every action is focused on business improvement.

> *Note: This meeting does not replace operational meetings. These typically take place weekly and focus on tasks, both those that happened or didn't happen last week and those that should happen next week.*

> ***"I have a great Board – we never argue."***

The words of a client who was CEO and major shareholder in a technology business. I had been introduced to him by his Operations Director. The Operations Director had contacted me because he was concerned about longer-term business performance; specifically, the challenges they were having executing on strategy.

I sat in on a couple of their management meetings and also talked to each Director separately. Some common issues emerged:

- There was a culture of actions being ignored.

- Each meeting generated a lot of actions.

- Each Director focused on their own function and did not feel able to (or want to) challenge and question other Directors.

- Everyone got on and there was never any disagreement in the meetings. Alternative views were quietly closed down by the CEO.

- One Director (who was not a shareholder and was a more recent hire) contributed little to the discussion and was not consulted on wider matters outside the meeting.

I worked with the CEO alone after the first couple of months. At one of our early meetings he expressed the view that he hired adults and he expected them to get on with their job without bothering him (he spent almost all his time on sales). At another meeting he uttered the words quoted above and seemed taken aback that I did not see this as a cause for celebration. He was disinclined to accept my suggestion that the role of a leader is to choose, motivate *and develop people, particularly the management team. He also struggled with the idea that constructive conflict might lead to the shared commitment so necessary in high-performing teams. He was unconvinced by the argument that even experienced people need a sense of purpose and belonging.*

Sometimes you can take a horse to water, but you can't make it a leader.

CHAPTER NINETEEN: SUCCESSFUL SYSTEMISATION

Systemisation in practice: DC, owner of a heating services company, says: "[systemisation]...helped us to develop our own strategy for managing every aspect of our business from sales and marketing to cashflow and work flow management. [...] helped us develop systems to manage the detail whilst maintaining the bigger picture. [...] Last year our turnover increased by 38%"

First the bad news. Systemisation doesn't always work. Across all the business owners I have worked with about one-third get it immediately and can take the trainer wheels off within a few months. Another third never get it and the assignment ends in tears. The final third are somewhere in the middle; it takes a bit longer, and lots of repetition and encouragement, before the lights start to go on.

I have obviously devoted much thought as to why this should be and have identified these critical success factors.

MANAGE TIME

Some business owners are unable to grasp the fact that they should be running their business, not the other way around. The systemisation activities that they know they should be working on to create the business they want get neglected because they are "too busy".

Business owners who succeed understand that:

1) The future is what they choose to make it.
2) They have a choice about the way they run their business and they make this choice every day.
3) A small investment of time sharpening their saw every day means they can cut down many more trees.
4) Business success is fundamentally about being organised.

At the risk of repeating myself, mindset change is the first and most important systemisation step.

Create space to routinely step back from your business and work on systemisation. Block out and protect a couple of days each month or half a day each week in your diary. For these periods, work somewhere where you are less likely to be interrupted and unable to interfere in daily operations. Nominate someone to run the business during these periods.

PLAN THE CHANGE

It is inevitable that when you start to introduce a change such as systemisation into a business you will meet with resistance from your employees.

Most of your employees will be comfortable with the way things are. They work willingly enough but if things go wrong, they feel no sense of responsibility – it's your company and your problem. After all, you must be making lots of money as the owner of the business.

Their reasons for coming to work are quite different from yours. As a good manager and leader, you of course try to engage them, develop them and reward them properly but no matter how good a manager you are, the majority of your workforce will feel little sense of ambition for someone else's business. It may also be the case that they feel little sense of ambition for themselves either, other than earning more. None of them will share your drive and frustration.

This gives you a problem.

You are trying to convince them of something that to you is perfectly logical and reasonable: In order to keep growing the business you need to run it differently, so you want employees to take more responsibility.

Yet to them this is threatening. Their activities are going to be documented. Their performance is going to be measured. They are going to be held accountable for their results. At best this means working harder; at worst it means that they will not be able to cut it and will lose their job as a result. No wonder they are resisting change.

Trying to make this change happen across the whole business at once can work if most of your direct reports and other employees are positive about your vision and clearly willing to take more responsibility. Often this happens where you have a lot of new staff or the whole business is young. Usually, however, you will have staff who are mostly opposed to change, or at best neutral. Overcoming this resistance in a single person is tough; if you give them the opportunity to form a group consensus in opposition it becomes very tough and some business owners give up, becoming a hostage to their employees.

One approach you can try to avoid this happening:

- Introduce the change to one part of the business at a time, starting with the most positive and willing of your direct reports. The idea is to a) avoid scaring people b) build a coalition of converts over time and c) avoid opportunities for a coalition of the reluctant to form. Once the first person is starting to work the new way then start on the next most positive and so on. Leave the assassins and energy-sappers till last
- Start by exposing each person you select to basic management information for their area in regular monthly reviews. Working through the numbers will lead to conversations about related KPIs and improvement plans.
- Involve them in developing the 12-month budget and KPI targets for their area.

- Over time adjust the balance of the monthly review to one where they are explaining performance and deciding actions and you are coaching them.
- Eventually each individual will be taking the responsibility you want them to and formalising it becomes a small step. Over time you build a coalition of the willing and accountability starts to become the norm in your business.

You might call this "Change by stealth". There are some drawbacks that immediately spring to mind:

- Time. With even a few managers this could take a couple of years. Surely it would be quicker to just tell everyone to start working the new way?
- What if you have no suitable people to start with?

To the first, the response must be that systemisation is not a simple, quick fix. It does take years and as developing and coaching your key people is going to become a large part of your job anyway, you might as well start now (see "Develop Your Managers" below)

The second is a tougher problem. If even the best of your people cannot or will not step up then you are faced with the risky and expensive prospect of hiring someone to replace them. This route should be avoided until you have first tried change by stealth –in many cases you will be pleasantly surprised. However, experience suggests that the team that got you from £0 to £1m will generally not be the same team that gets you from £1m to £10m, who will generally not be the same team that gets you from £10m to £100m. You need to be prepared for some people voting with their feet. Whilst unsettling and inconvenient when it happens it usually indicates that you are making progress.

DEVELOP YOUR MANAGERS

As your business grows you become more and more of a bottleneck. No matter how many hours you work, and how many staff you hire, the things that only you know how to do, and the decisions that only you know how to make, become the things that slow everything else down and your business growth will tail off.

You must find a way to get things done through others. You must develop a management team who can run the day-to-day while you focus once again on growing the business.

Once you master delegation it makes your business scalable.

What are the challenges?

I have described why many of your employees will feel uncomfortable about the changes you need to make to your business to continue growing and may resist change as a result. This applies to your managers as well. They may feel more threatened by the changes than most employees. They may not currently be called managers, or think of themselves as managers, or understand what managers are supposed to do.

It is usual as you consider the way you want the business to be in future to worry that you don't have the right people to step up and take on more responsibility. Perhaps they are not displaying the drive or commercial awareness that you would like, or perhaps they seem to avoid taking responsibility. It may be that the people who got you to this point aren't the people who will get you to your vision. They may not have the ability or attitude to step up. However, it could be that you do have the right people – it's just that the way you have run the business so far has not allowed them to show what they can do.

Figure 46 shows a way of thinking about the performance of your managers.

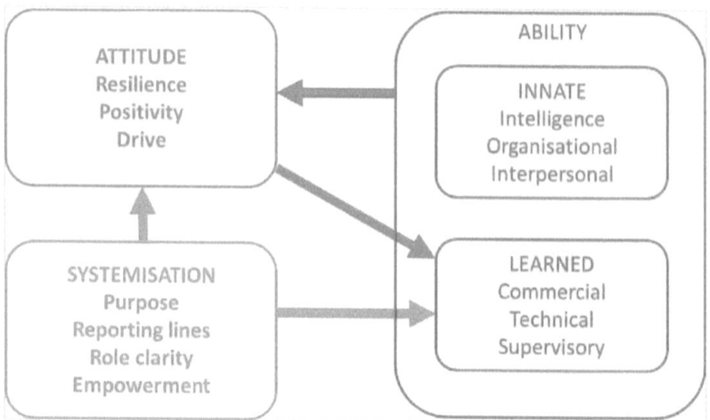

Figure 46 - Manager Performance Framework

Your managers will have some innate ability levels. You will be largely wasting your time if you attempt to improve any of these.

They will also have some learned abilities that can be improved under the right circumstances:

- The person concerned must have a desire to learn and improve (they must have the right attitude).
- The organisation must provide an environment that encourages learning. Improvement must result in rewards that matter to the person concerned and the necessary structure, purpose, measurements, support and resources must be provided (in short, the business must be systemised).

A manager's attitude is largely innate. You will be wasting your time trying to impart drive to someone who is habitually lazy, or a positive mindset to someone who is naturally gloomy. What is easy to achieve, however, is the reverse of this. If you put someone who is naturally positive and hard-working in a role where:

- they feel out of their depth (they are working beyond their ability), or
- they do not have clear goals, authority and performance feedback (the organisational environment is poor; that is, the business is not systemised)

then their attitude will rapidly deteriorate.

A systemised business has a shared vision, clear role definitions, unambiguous objectives, empowerment, and appropriate delegated authority. It also includes the way you manage; such factors as:

- Effective, regular two-way communication.
- Consistent, calm and steady leadership in pursuit of the plan.
- Fair and evidence-based decisions.

> *Note: It is very difficult to lead change and develop your management team if you do not start with their respect. If you find yourself in this unfortunate position you may have to settle for the status-quo, unless you are prepared to change the people.*

Your scope for action is therefore limited when it comes to transforming your managers into the people who are going to run your business for you:

Step 1. If the environment is not conducive to high-performance (if the business is not systemised) then systemise it.

Step 2. If the business is systemised and you believe a particular under-performance is due to a deficiency in a learned ability, then agree a personal development plan to overcome this.

Step 3. If any under-performance remains then find a different role they can do well, or if no such role exists dismiss them, and put someone else in their place, either promoting internally or by recruiting someone.

You can use a tool such as that shown in Figure 47 to assess the potential of your managers.

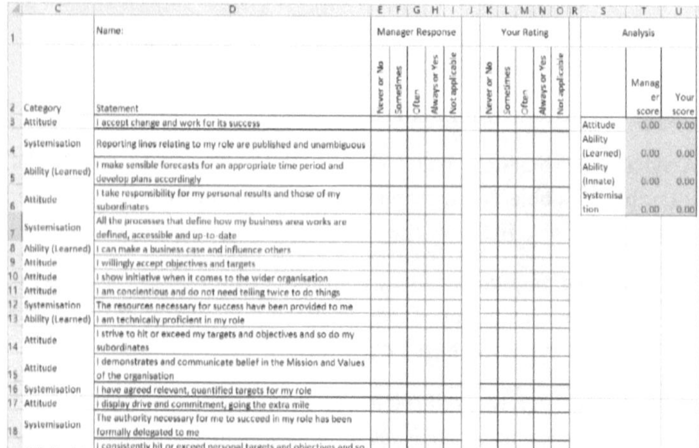

	Category	Statement	Manager Response					Your Rating						Analysis		
1		Name:	Never or No	Sometimes	Often	Always or Yes	Not applicable	Never or No	Sometimes	Often	Always or Yes	Not applicable			Manager score	Your score
2	Category	Statement														
3	Attitude	I accept change and work for its success												Attitude	0.00	0.00
4	Systemisation	Reporting lines relating to my role are published and unambiguous												Ability (Learned)	0.00	0.00
5	Ability (Learned)	I make sensible forecasts for an appropriate time period and develop plans accordingly												Ability (Innate)	0.00	0.00
6	Attitude	I take responsibility for my personal results and those of my subordinates												Systemisation	0.00	0.00
7	Systemisation	All the processes that define how my business area works are defined, accessible and up-to-date														
8	Ability (Learned)	I can make a business case and influence others														
9	Attitude	I willingly accept objectives and targets														
10	Attitude	I show initiative when it comes to the wider organisation														
11	Attitude	I am concientious and do not need telling twice to do things														
12	Systemisation	The resources necessary for success have been provided to me														
13	Ability (Learned)	I am technically proficient in my role														
14	Attitude	I strive to hit or exceed my targets and objectives and so do my subordinates														
15	Attitude	I demonstrates and communicate belief in the Mission and Values of the organisation														
16	Systemisation	I have agreed relevant, quantified targets for my role														
17	Attitude	I display drive and commitment, going the extra mile														
18	Systemisation	The authority necessary for me to succeed in my role has been formally delegated to me														
	Ability (Innate)	I consistently hit or exceed personal targets and objectives and so														

Figure 47 – Example Manager Assessment Tool

MAKE THINGS ROUTINE

Some business owners manage to make the necessary systemisation changes but then fail to make the new way of running their business routine and resilient. If they get busy or get hit by unexpected events, good or bad, they revert to the old reactive way of doing things. Meetings and performance reviews get missed, corners get cut.

Business owners who succeed embed systemisation into their business so that it becomes the natural, habitual way to do things. Whatever happens, they still run their business in an organised, planned way. They understand that all of the work invested in getting your staff to think differently and work differently can be undone in a few moments if their employees sense that the boss does not believe in it and abandons it at the first sniff of difficulty.

If you don't truly believe that the way to scale up a successful business is by taking an organised, planned approach to running it no matter what then no-one else is going to believe it.

REVIEW PERFORMANCE

Some business owners identify what they need to measure, set targets and make individual employees responsible for hitting those targets – but then never review performance.

You can explain a target. You can agree with someone they are responsible for it. But until you regularly review performance against targets you don't make it real for the people concerned.

Business owners who succeed recognise that systemisation is at heart about transforming what their employees believe about the business and their role in it. If performance is never reviewed against a target, then the employee concerned will rightly conclude that it wasn't important after all.

If you don't truly believe that the way to scale up a successful business is by making employees responsible for results and working with them to help them succeed, then no-one else is going to believe it.

GET HELP

Almost anything in life worth doing requires training and coaching. If you want to be great at a sport or playing a musical instrument, then you need a coach or tutor.

If you want to qualify as a doctor or a lawyer, you don't achieve this by just reading books. This might sound strange from someone who has written a book about changing your business; the point is that studying a subject this way is necessary but not sufficient to implement successful change.

Yet when it comes to learning how to run a growing business people are often quite prepared to just "have a go" or "learn on the job" - even though running a business brings far more challenges than playing a guitar or hitting a golf ball (neither of these things answer back, oversleep, get sick, fail to listen or fall out with each other).

My golf pro can watch my swing and then tell me that I am moving my head or not shifting my weight properly. My guitar tutor can watch me play and tell me that my wrist is moving, or that I am using the wrong fingering. Neither of these things is apparent to me - either that they are happening or even that they are a bad thing. This problem has been described by Noel Burch as the four stages of learning (Burch, 1970), where someone must move from unconsciously incompetent (blissful ignorance) through consciously incompetent (I know there is something wrong but not how to fix it), consciously competent (I can do this but I need to think about it each time) to unconsciously competent

(I have mastered the skill). This requires an objective viewpoint, pattern recognition and a toolkit of previous solutions to improve someone's execution of a task – everything you get from a coach.

Studies (The Alternative Board, 2015), (Cogent Research and Analysis Ltd, 2011), (Leonard-Cross, 2010) have shown the benefits of business coaching are real. I look at some reasons why business owners don't use coaches in the next (and final) chapter. However, as the old saying (sort of) goes "If you think it is expensive to hire a professional, wait until you try using an amateur (or doing it yourself)".

EPILOGUE: RETURN TO SMITHS WIDGETS

Systemisation in practice: CB, owner of an event management business, says: "We now manage a more organised company with time to forward plan and if problems do arise, we have systems in place to manage them. [...] our total sales have increased by 20.4%."

When we left John, he was not enjoying running his business but had pretty much given up any thoughts of changing the way things were.

He had resigned himself to long hours, needy staff and stalled growth. He comforted himself with the thought that all this came with the territory and was the lot of every business owner. He put down the continued growth of some other businesses to luck; maybe they hired the right person or landed the right customer.

His frustration and ambition were only just below the surface, however, and it didn't take much to wake them. He received an email inviting him to an event on business systemisation – the kind of thing he deleted immediately normally but this seemed to be aimed exactly at him. He and Andrew talked about it, agreed that it was probably a con and they didn't have time to attend anyway.

A few months later he received another email on the same topic. Again, it managed to describe his situation perfectly. A couple of staff had resigned recently, and a big customer was making noises about re tendering their contract. His business felt fragile. This time he decided to attend – if not with an open mind exactly, at least determined to try and get some value from it and then block any future emails.

On the day he and Andrew learned a lot. It turned out that their way of running a business wasn't the only way (although the room was filled with business owners who had the same problems as they did). Some business owners had found a way to break out of the trap. They had applied some simple rules and techniques to their business so that their employees did all the doing while they, the business owners, grew the business. After the event they agreed to meet up with the presenter to discuss their business and see whether systemisation could help.

At the first meeting they learned quite a lot more about how systemisation could help them think about their business differently and run it differently. They still had some pretty serious doubts though.

- Cost. With the business marking time how could they justify paying a consultant's fees for what could be 6 to 12 months? The consultant agreed that the fees would seem high – if they did nothing with the guidance they were given. If, on the other hand, they managed to break out of their current situation and started to bring in some of the deals that their product ought to then in a year or two the resulting business growth and peace of mind would make the fees seem vanishingly small.

- Efficacy. How could they be sure that systemisation worked at all let alone for their business, which was (of course) completely different to every other business in the world? The consultant said that success was not guaranteed but that the methodology, techniques and tools used had been proven to work by the many business owners who had systemised their business – many of them documented in case studies. Historically it failed in about one-third of cases – the main variable being the business owners themselves.

- Time. They were flat out running the business now, so it seemed unlikely that they would be able to find the time to "do systemisation" as well – so they felt there was a good chance that they would end up as one of the one-third failures. The consultant agreed that if they didn't find a way to manage their time better then failure was pretty much a given – but that firstly, techniques to help them to manage their time better were usually an early deliverable of the approach and secondly, letting the business run them was a choice not a given.

- Ability. John and Andrew were worried that trying to systemise their business would simply expose their own shortcomings when it came to leadership and management. What if they didn't understand stuff? What if they led and no-one followed? The consultant responded that if they did not have the respect of their employees then change (or anything else) would be difficult. Other than that, the skills and techniques required are simple to learn and the process is one of working with employees rather than having to urge them forward through sheer force of personality and rousing speeches.

They decided to change.

In their first session they documented their objectives – the tangible things they wanted to change in their business. Using the Systemisation Roadmap they identified priorities; those areas where they could get most benefit quickest. They decided that the business imperative was to learn how to consistently bring in more business – to create a marketing and sales process. It was pretty easy to agree realistic targets for this. However, to achieve the change they needed to free up their time and protect that time even as the business got busier. This meant that they needed to start with the "Who" leg and pass responsibility for operations to someone else. This gave them a sequence – an action plan.

In the second session they reviewed and confirmed their targets and plan. They drafted their as-is and to-be Organisation Charts and created a couple of job descriptions, choosing roles that covered the things they wanted to delegate early to free up time for business development.

By the third session they had discussed these things with their staff and asked them all to draft their own job description using a standard template. During the session they worked through the Delegation Planner and had a go at mapping their sales process.

That's where we leave John and Andrew. Will it work? Well, to an extent it has worked already; they have acknowledged that there is a better way to run their business, defined how they are going to change and what their objectives are and made the giant leap of starting to change things on the ground. However, systemisation in their business is still a fragile plant. Will it survive the gales of operational problems and overload? Can they protect it from the frosts of employee scepticism and passive resistance? Will they be able to permanently change the way they think about their business and their self-image?

If they do, then they will have broken out of the business owners' trap and they will start to reap the rewards that all their hard work deserves.

SYSTEMISATION RESOURCES AND SUPPORT

Systemisation in practice: SC, owner of a software development company, says: "[systemisation]...helped me to create the proper scaffolding required for the smooth running of a rapidly developing business. Using a more systemised approach releases me from sinking beneath the weight of too many different demands and thereby allows me to run a rapidly growing business and to focus on business development."

All the resources used in this book can be downloaded from http://www.nickbettes.co.uk/books/unchain-your-business/

You can enroll on a complete and cost-effective online coaching course that provides video and coaching support through all the systemisation stages in this book at the same website address.

You can contact me about 121 or group systemisation coaching at unchained@nickbettes.co.uk

If you are a business coach or consultant who would like to know more about systemisation and add it to your service portfolio then visit www.businesscoachkit.com

Bibliography

Adair, J. (1988). *The Action-Centred Leader*. Spiro Press.

Anyadike-Danes, H. B. (2010). Who Creates the Jobs? *Significance (Royal Statistical Society)*.

Burch, N. (1970). *Four Stages for Learning Any New Skill*. Gordon Training International.

Cogent Research and Analysis Ltd. (2011). *SME Business Performance & The Impact of Business Coaching Study*. Cogent Research and Analysis Ltd.

Gawande, A. (2011). *The Checklist Manifesto*. Profile Books Limited.

Harnish, V. (2014). *Scaling Up*. Gazelles Inc.

Hart, M., & Anyadike-Danes, M. (2014). *Moving on from the 'Vital 6%'*. Enterprise Research Centre.

Lencioni, P. (2005). *The Five Dysfunctions of a Team*. Jossey-Bass.

Leonard-Cross, E. (2010). Developmental coaching: Business benefit – fact or fad? An evaluative study to explore the impact of coaching in the workplace. *International Coaching Psychology Review Vol. 5 No. 1*.

The Alternative Board. (2015). *Small Business Pulse Survey*. The Alternative Board.

Wageman, R., Nunes, D., Burruss, J., & Hackman, J. (2008). *Senior Leadership Teams: What it Takes to Make Them Great*. Harvard Business School Publishing Corporation.